Miracles

EYEWITNESSES *to Some of the*
GREATEST MIRACLES *of Our Time*

Miracles

R.W. SCHAMBACH

DESTINY IMAGE® PUBLISHERS, INC.

P.O. Box 310, Shippensburg, PA 17257-0310
"Speaking to the Purposes of God for this Generation and for the Generations to Come."

This book and all other Destiny Image, Revival Press, Mercy Place, Fresh Bread, Destiny Image Fiction, and Treasure House books are available at Christian bookstores and distributors worldwide.

For a U.S. bookstore nearest you, call 1-800-722-6774.
For more information on foreign distributors, call 717-532-3040.
Or reach us on the Internet: www.destinyimage.com

ISBN 10: 0-7684-2830-0   ISBN 13: 978-0-7684-2830-8

For Worldwide Distribution, Printed in the U.S.A.
1 2 3 4 5 6 7 8 9 10 11 / 13 12 11 10 09

Miracles Previous ISBN 0-89274-811-7
Copyright © 1993 by R. W. Schambach
Miracles 2: Greater Miracles
Previous ISBN 1-888361-52-2
Copyright © 2003 by R.W. Schambach

Table of Contents

PART III
MIRACLES OF HEALING

PART IV

FINANCIAL MIRACLES

Foreword

Most of my life I have heard the stories that Brother Schambach tells. Some of the miracles that you are about to read, I have heard a hundred times!

I will read this book right along with you. No matter how often I hear my husband tell them, they are always fresh. They demonstrate the miracle-working power of God.

Brother Schambach began his evangelistic ministry in 1955 while working with renowned evangelist Brother A. A. Allen, from whom he received valuable training. This prepared him for the work God had called him to.

In 1959, Brother Schambach began his ministry with a crusade in Newark, New Jersey, where signs and wonders followed. The revival lasted for six months! Reluctant to leave the new converts and friends, he founded a church, Newark Miracle Temple.

This pattern was repeated as Brother Schambach traveled across the East. Later on, other Miracle Temple churches were established in

Philadelphia, Chicago, and Brooklyn. His reputation became that of one of the great "tent evangelists."

Across the country, Brother Schambach held great revivals under his ministry's tent, where virtually thousands of lost souls came to Christ. Thousands more received physical, financial, and emotional miracles. Brother Schambach's radio broadcasts and television program soon became powerful extensions of the ministry with which God had blessed him.

Today the same signs and wonders still follow Brother Schambach's work. The pages of this book relate some of those miracles.

Many of the miracles you are going to read in this book took place while I was standing right beside Brother Schambach; I am an eyewitness to them. For instance, you will read about the 17 deaf and dumb brothers and sisters in Africa. All of them were healed and began to hear and speak in one miracle service!

It is exciting to be there when God's power is at work. Because Brother Schambach is a powerful storyteller, you will feel as if you were really there with him. He brings the stories to life, making them vivid and alive.

I have watched little children sit spellbound with their eyes wide and their mouths open as Brother Schambach tells a story. He has a unique and fascinating way of expressing himself.

I hope that the miracle stories included in this book will build your faith and inspire you as you continue to walk with the Lord.

"Winn" Schambach

"I Believe in Miracles"

I believe in miracles!

If you cut all the miracles out of the Bible, you would not have a Bible left. It's a book of the miraculous, because our God is a miracle-working God. And my Bible declares that He is the same yesterday, today, and forever! You know what that means? It means He is still doing today what He did yesterday. He's still doing the miraculous! In fact, I believe we are going to see greater miracles in these last days than we have ever seen before.

Jesus began His public ministry as a ministry of miracles. Everything about His life involved miracles: His conception, birth, life, wisdom and teachings, ministry, death, resurrection, appearances, and ascension—all of these were astounding and undeniable miracles.

Jesus always attracted the multitudes by His miracles then, and He does so today, wherever miracles are done in His name. If we preach as the early Church preached, we will get the same results that they got: miracles and healings. It doesn't matter where we are or who we are. If we want to get Bible results, we have to preach what the Bible says: that miracles are a part of the present-day ministry of Jesus Christ.

Some folks don't believe this. They say the days of miracles are over. You can even hear this from the pulpit. Some preachers say that the miraculous was only for the early Church. Many people have said that miracles were just for the days of the Old and New Testaments, but that is not true. God has not changed. He is the same yesterday, today, and forever. He is still in the miracle business. Jesus Christ is as much a miracle-worker now as He ever was, and people need His miracle touch now more than ever.

We are called to walk as the Christians did in the New Testament, to serve the needs of people today. Jesus must be allowed to live in us, in His power and with His personal presence guiding us.

When people act on God's Word in bold faith, the faith that produces miracles, then multitudes come from miles around, eager to see Christ's miracle power in demonstration.

The power of God is real today just like it was 2,000 years ago. I've seen hundreds of miracles with my own eyes—people being healed and set free by the power of the living Christ!

I get so many letters, phone calls, and e-mails from people who have received miracles from God. In my meetings, people come back to testify of how the Lord touched their lives. It blesses my heart to hear these stories of what God has done. I like to share them with the world, to let people know that God is not dead, but He is alive, and He's doing great things in all the earth. That is the reason for this book—to let the world know what the Lord has done.

Unfortunately, some Christians aren't aware of the power of God that is available to us as believers. A.J. Gordon, a theologian, once declared, "The Church is losing her grip on the supernatural." Too often all we see is a manifestation of the flesh and an emphasis on man's ability—what man has learned.

Yet there is something crying out of every believer today—"I want to see a miracle! I want to see the supernatural!"

God is looking for the believer to take up his or her responsibility—to be obedient to His voice and help release God's miracle power. When we come to the place where we move on what God says, when He says it, miracles will become a way of life.

What do you have need of? You can pinpoint it. Maybe you need a healing in your body. Maybe your back is against the wall financially. Maybe you have a son who is hooked on drugs, bound by the devil, or a daughter who has run away from home. I don't care what the need is; God will perform a miracle in your life.

Your family may say you are crazy for believing God for a miracle. Your friends may look at you funny. Even your preacher may tell you that God doesn't work miracles anymore. Just let them talk. Let every man and let every devil be a liar, but let God be true! If He said it, He will do it! And if He spoke it, He will bring it to pass. No ifs, ands, buts, or maybes.

If you abide in Me, and My words abide in you, you will ask what you desire, and it shall be done for you. By this My Father is glorified, that you bear much fruit; so you will be My disciples… You did not choose Me, but I chose you and appointed you that you should go and bear fruit, and that your fruit should remain, that whatever you ask the Father in My name He may give you (John 15:7-8,16).

Do you believe it? I'm telling you, folks, God's power works! If it didn't work, I would not have been in this for so long. I'd have done something else. But I cannot deny the power of God at work in the lives of people today—and when you read this book, you won't be able to either.

In this book, I want to teach you what I have learned throughout my many years of ministry about the miracle-working power of God, and I want to share with you some of the most amazing miracles I have witnessed. As you read, let faith come alive in your heart, and get ready to receive your miracle!

PART I

The ANATOMY of a *Miracle*

The Anatomy of a Miracle

On the third day there was a wedding in Cana of Galilee, and the mother of Jesus was there. Now both Jesus and His disciples were invited to the wedding. And when they ran out of wine, the mother of Jesus said to Him, "They have no wine." Jesus said to her, "Woman, what does your concern have to do with Me? My hour has not yet come." His mother said to the servants, "Whatever He says to you, do it."

Now there were set there six waterpots of stone, according to the manner of purification of the Jews, containing twenty or thirty gallons apiece. Jesus said to them, "Fill the waterpots with water." And they filled them up to the brim. And He said to them, "Draw some out now, and take it to the master of the feast." And they took it. When the master of the feast had tasted the water that was made wine, and did not know where it came from (but the servants who had drawn the water knew), the master of the feast called the bridegroom. And he said to him, "Every man at the beginning sets out the good wine, and when the guests have well drunk, then the inferior. You have kept the good wine until now!"

This beginning of signs Jesus did in Cana of Galilee, and manifested His glory; and His disciples believed in Him (John 2:1-11).

The key to receiving a miracle from God is found in the second chapter of John's Gospel, in one of the most familiar stories in the whole Bible, the turning of water into wine. You should have verse 5 underscored in your Bible. It says, "His mother said to the servants, 'Whatever He says to you, do it.'"

This is the very first miracle Jesus performed that we know about. It wasn't a blind eye that He opened. It wasn't a sick man who He healed. It happened when He was invited to a wedding. There is something more significant to this story than what we've always been taught. This event was not just for Jesus to place His approbation on the institution of marriage. I believe there is a deeper truth Jesus is trying to get across to everyone in His Church. He wants us to see that the uniting of personal faith with Christ produces God's power to bring forth a miracle. You have something to do with it as an individual. Don't put it all off on God.

Many times we say, "I believe God will do it in His own time"— and totally overlook the fact that God is waiting for us to do something. There's a human responsibility that must accede to the divine sovereignty of God in order to produce the miracle. But there's something you've got to do.

Thank God we are living in a day of miracles.

When I go to church, I want to see a demonstration of the power of God. The Bible says God is a spirit, and they who worship Him must worship Him in spirit and in truth (see John 4:24). Paul, writing in the second book of Timothy, said the church had a form of godliness but was denying the power of God. He said to turn away from such practices.

Perhaps you have been involved in a cold, dead, formal church that offers nothing but a form, a ceremony, and a ritual. God said to

turn away from it. It's about time that the Church produces the supernatural and the miraculous.

THE MIRACLE WORKER

You're not serving a dead Christ, but a risen Savior! Some still try
to keep Him on a cross, but I want you to know Jesus came off that
cross. They put Him in a grave, but He came out of the grave. Jesus is
alive! He's the same today as He was yesterday, and He's still performing miracles.

Hebrews 2:1-4 says:

> *Therefore we must give the more earnest heed to the things
> which we have heard, lest we drift away. For if the word spoken
> through angels proved steadfast, and every transgression and
> disobedience received a just reward, how shall we escape if we
> neglect so great a salvation, which at the first began to be spoken
> by the Lord, and was confirmed to us by those who heard Him,
> God also bearing witness both with signs and wonders, with
> various miracles, and gifts of the Holy Spirit, according to His
> own will?*

God is the God of the miraculous. This Gospel that we preach is
good news about the supernatural. It's a Gospel of power. When I
preach, I want to see God move in a miraculous way where people
can receive what they've come for. Hallelujah!

In John 3:2, Nicodemus, making reference to the wedding at Cana,
said, "No one can do these signs that You do unless God is with him."
Jesus' ministry was earmarked with miracles. He is the Miracle-
Worker, and He's alive today showing forth signs and wonders and
miracles. He's the same today as He was yesterday. Hallelujah!

There are 16 recorded miracles of healing in the
Gospels...miracles that Jesus himself performed. There were three
people raised from the dead, not counting His own resurrection;
three exorcisms where He cast the devil out of people; and six mira-

cles over the forces of nature. I'm talking about a Miracle-Worker. Yet all we're doing today is playing church…having a form, a ceremony, and a ritual.

I declare unto you that my God is not dead. My God is alive! He's the same yesterday, He's the same today, and He'll be the same tomorrow. He is a God of the miraculous and the supernatural.

YOU MUST DO YOUR PART

Jesus turned water into wine. It was the beginning of His miracles. But there had to be an association—a cooperation—of Christ with people. *Whatever He says to you, do it.* God wants you to cooperate with Him. Be obedient to do what He tells you to do, and then you will see miracles take place.

When the preacher says, "Rise up and walk!"—get up and start walking, and you'll have your miracle.

We're the Church. But we've been sitting back saying, "Well, I'm just waiting on the Lord. When the Lord gets ready to hand out a miracle, I'm going to receive it."

With that attitude, you're going to die waiting. You're not waiting on God. God's waiting on you.

I was preaching in Philadelphia one year where six people in wheelchairs were lined up in the front row—just listening to my sermon. They hadn't walked in a dozen years or so, and while I was preaching, God began to work miracles. I didn't even lay hands on those people and pray for them. He beat me to it. Five of them got up and started running. I wasn't concerned about those five; I was after the one still in his wheelchair.

I ran down to him, and I said, "Get up!"

He said, "I can't walk."

I said, "No kidding. Now get up in the name of Jesus!"

"Oh," he said, "the doctors said I'd never walk again."

Here five men sitting next to him got up out of their wheelchairs, and he's still sitting in his. I wanted him to get up. I reached down and yanked him out of the thing.

I said again, "Get out of it!"

He stood up and said, "Whoo, I haven't done this in years."

I'm a man—men can't perform miracles. God performs miracles, but He is looking for human responsibility, blended with this Word, to produce miracle power. *Whatever He says to you, do it.*

Don't hesitate. Be obedient to Him.

As we examine the teachings of Jesus, we find there are six principles He sets forth on how to see a miracle. These conditions are always present when God's miracle power is manifested.

CHAPTER 1

The Area of Faith

Where does faith work? The first miracle principle is that we must identify the area where a miracle is needed and therefore is possible. This is the area of faith. The second chapter of John tells us there wasn't any wine left at the wedding in Cana. That was the area of faith. Someone may say, "The doctor has given up on me." Oh, hallelujah, it's about time. That's that person's area of faith.

Suppose a woman says, "My husband told me he's going to leave." That's not the area of faith. But when she says, "He's gone," then she can also say, "Oh, now God's going to move!" This is when faith moves—this is the area of faith.

As long as they had wine at the wedding feast, Jesus didn't need to perform a miracle. But when they ran out, He said, "Now, watch and see what I'm going to do."

People may say, "All I've got left is a dollar. I'd better hang onto it." That's wrong thinking! They'll never get anything if they don't turn it loose. They have to be reduced to an irreducible minimum until it seems they have nothing. Then, when their back is against the wall, they are standing in the place where faith begins to move and the supernatural takes over. Then God will perform a miracle. The Bible says there was no wine at Cana. They had reached the place of frustration—the place where faith begins.

NO PLACE ELSE TO GO

Perhaps you are at the point of frustration.

Jesus met people who were in this place, frustrated, with "no wine," who had nothing left. All through the Word of God there are examples of this. When you are on the brink of natural extremity, you've reached the place of divine intervention. When there's no more hope, God says, "Now it's time for Me to step in!"

I want to encourage you. I don't care what the doctors told you. Don't believe their report. There's only one report to believe. God said in Isaiah 53:1, *"Who has believed our report? And to whom has the arm of the Lord been revealed?"* (What is the report?) He also said, *"He was wounded for our transgressions, He was bruised for our iniquities; the chastisement for our peace was upon him, and by His stripes we are healed"* (Isaiah 53:5). We are healed. That's what I believe. That is the only message I believe. It's the only report that I believe. Let every man be a liar. Let every devil be a liar. But let God be true. If He said it, He will do it, and if He spoke it, He's going to bring it to pass.

PUTTING BACK WHAT WAS TAKEN

First Samuel 30 tells about David at Ziklag. He and his soldiers came home and found everything gone—his wife, everything. David was a man of God, but he backslid. I believe that only good should follow the people of God, but here everything's messed up. He came back and all of his soldier's loved ones were gone. The Amalekites had destroyed the city; I mean they had raped the entire village. Not only did David have to deal with that, but his followers also wanted to stone him for allowing this to happen.

So David found a priest. And he said to the priest, "It's time to seek the Lord." David prayed, "Lord, I'm outnumbered. Do you want me to go get them?" And God said, "Go get them and you'll recover everything that was taken." Oh, I love that!

Hear me, beloved. I don't care what the devil's stolen from you; God's going to let you recover everything. Isn't that good news?

Someone may say, "Oh, if I could have just heard this three years ago, before I had the operation." Well, it's never too late with God. He'll put back what the doctors took out. A lady came to one of my services who had had a hysterectomy, and all of her female organs had been removed. She heard me preach one night and came forward for a prayer. She said, "Lay your hands on me. Ask God to put back in what the doctor took out. I want a baby." I laid hands on her, and I said, "In the name of Jesus, I command you to bring forth a child in nine months." That's cutting it close. A year later she came through the prayer line, held the baby up in front of me, and said, "Here he is. God put back in what the doctors took out!" It's never too late with God!

I want to encourage you—God is a God of the miraculous and the supernatural. All He's looking for is a little cooperation on your part. He just wants you to believe.

In Mark 5:26, there's a story of a little woman who spent all she had. She finally arrived in the area of faith. Oh, thank God, she spent it all. (See, nobody said anything when she spent it all on doctors. But if she had given it all to a preacher, all hell would have broken loose!) The Bible says this little woman *"had spent all that she had and was no better, but rather grew worse."* She came to where Jesus was and said, "He doesn't have to lay His hands on me. Just let me get close enough to where He is, and let me touch the hem of His garment." Are you following me?

She pressed through that crowd until all of a sudden she saw that white robe. She reached out and touched one little piece of it, and Jesus stopped instantly. He stood there and said, "Who touched Me?"

The disciples answered, "What do you mean, who touched you? They've all got their hands on You!" And Jesus said, "I know it, but somebody touched Me with faith." Oh, hallelujah! She felt it in her body—she was healed of her plague.

You don't have to have someone tell you you're healed when the power of God comes in your body. You'll be the first one to know that you are healed.

IN POSITION FOR A MIRACLE

Look at John 20:19—oh, I like this one. *"Then, the same day at evening, being the first day of the week, when the doors were shut where the disciples were assembled, for fear of the Jews, Jesus came and stood in the midst…."* He came when all hope was gone. This is when He comes. This is the area of faith, when there is no hope left. The doors are shut, in the evening hour, the darkest time of your life. Many of you are there right now.

You may say, "Brother Schambach, you don't know what I'm going through." Dry those tears, beloved, you're in the area of faith. You are ripe for a miracle. "But you don't know what the doctor said." I don't have to know what the doctor said; I just know what God said.

This is the first principle, getting to the area of faith. You must identify with it.

CHAPTER 2

The Author of Faith

Now, look at the second principle—know the Author of faith. You can't miss when you know the Author. You want to find out who the Author of faith is?

John 2:5 says the mother of Jesus was at the wedding. Am I trying to say that Mary is the author of faith? You would think so from what some churches say. No, no, no! A thousand times, no! Mary is not the author of faith! Mary's the one who said, "Whatever He says to you, do it!" Thank God for Mary, who had enough sense to point people to the One who is the Author of faith. Jesus is the Answer— Jesus is the Way. Thank God for Mary, who birthed that Man. But Jesus is the Author of faith.

Hebrews 12:2 says, *"Looking unto Jesus, the author and finisher of our faith...."* If you're going to get a miracle, get your eyes off Buddha. Get your eyes off Mohammed. Get your eyes off Mary. Get your eyes off religion. And get your eyes on Jesus Christ. Behold the Lamb of God who takes away the sin of the world! He is the Author of faith.

It's a dangerous thing to follow a man. If you follow a man, you'll end up like those hundreds of followers of Jim Jones in Guyana who facilitated mass suicide. Following a man like Jim Jones will lead you into hell. By the same token, you've got no right following an evangelist. You've got no right following a pastor or even a church. Get your eyes on Jesus Christ, who is the Author and Finisher of your faith. If you get your eyes on a man you'll become disillusioned. Man will fail you. Man will let you down. Man will disappoint you, but Jesus Christ will never disappoint you because He is the Author of your faith. Jesus is the object of our worship.

THE WAY TO A MIRACLE…IS JESUS!

Do you remember when Jesus came to His disciples, walking on water? (See Matthew 14:22-33.) He had told them, "Get into a boat and go to the other side and I'll meet you over there." Then He spent some time in prayer to His Father. When He got done praying, the last boat had already left.

Oh, I could preach a whole message on this one. But what He says, He's got to do. If He doesn't do it, He's not God. Are you with me? That's why you need to study the Word and find out what He says. If He said it, He'll do it, and if He spoke it, He'll bring it to pass.

He said, "I'll meet you on the other side." There's only one thing left for Him to do—start walking on the water. And guess what? He caught up to the boat! The disciples were looking out over the edge of the boat, and all of a sudden they saw Him coming. And they got scared! Of what? The supernatural!

Oh, that's why the Church doesn't have the supernatural! Have you ever gotten scared in church? No, you sit there in those cushioned seats, get lullabied to sleep—you know what's going to happen before it happens. If Jesus had come to the disciples in a boat, they would have just sat there and gone to sleep. But He came in a different way. He came walking on the water.

The disciples said, "Look, it's His ghost!" They already had Him dead. Just like the Church—they're always saying God's dead. One of them said, "That isn't Him; nobody can walk on water." Yes, that was Him! Peter said, "Hold it, fellows. I know one surefire way to tell whether it's Him or not. Hey, Lord Jesus.... Hey, is that You out there?" I like ol' Peter. He said, "Lord, if that's You, tell me to come out there where You are."

Jesus said, "Come." One word. Peter didn't hesitate. He took those big size twelves out of the boat and put them right on the water. And he walked on the water! It was a miracle! Peter walked on water. Jesus walked on water. Peter was uniting his own human responsibility with the Word of Jesus Christ, and it produced a miracle.

Somebody says, "Yeah, but he sank." In order to sink, you've got to be on top! He walked on the water. As long as Peter had his eyes on the Author of faith, he had it made.

DON'T GET DISTRACTED

The moment Peter took his eyes off Jesus, he saw the waves, the wind, and the sea as it began to rage. He got distracted, just like when you say, "Jesus is my Healer"—and then you get a pain around the fifth rib on the left side. You know what I mean! As long as he had his eyes on Jesus, the miracle was sure. But the moment he was distracted, fear, doubt, and unbelief settled in.

Jesus said, "Oh, ye of little faith, why did you doubt?" Who's He talking to? Peter...the big fisherman. He doubted Jesus. Every one of us knows what it's like to doubt Jesus.

He said, "Oh, ye of little faith." Well, at least Peter had a little faith. If he had a little faith, how much did the rest of those boys inside the boat have? At least Peter got his feet wet.

You are "playing church" if you're in the boat. Get out of the boat and learn how to trust God! Jesus is the Author of faith. Today is your day for a miracle. But there's a part you have to play.

CHAPTER 3

The Attitude of Faith

I want you to know that John 2:5 is a faith trigger—*Whatever He says to you, do it.* This is the crux of faith. God is looking for obedience. You show me a man or a woman with faith, and I'll show you a man and a woman who knows how to obey God. *Whatever He says to you, do it.* This is the right attitude—the attitude of faith. What you receive from God depends a lot on your attitude.

We always put the responsibility on God, and say, "Well, when He gets ready, He's going to come by where I live." But I tell you He's been ready for almost 2,000 years, and you're going to have to change your attitude to receive a miracle from God.

The attitude of faith requires personal initiative on our part. The Bible says that before Jesus performed that first miracle, He was called (see John 2:2). Remember that! He will not force Himself on anybody. You're the one who is going to have to initiate your requests.

It's the same way with salvation. Jesus Christ will never come to your house unless you initiate an invitation first. He said, "...the one who comes *to Me I will by no means cast out*" (John 6:37). The Bible says, *"If we confess our sins, He is faithful and just to forgive us our sins and to cleanse us from all unrighteousness"* (1 John 1:9). He comes only by invitation.

The invitation you extend to Jesus must be by your personal initiative and express your personal desire. The scripture says the guests at the wedding feast wanted wine. They had no wine, and they set out to get some. Well, how badly do you want something from God? How badly do you want to be healed? How badly do you want to be delivered and set free? How much do you really want it?

God wants you to have desires like David had. David said, *"As the deer pants for the water brooks, so pants my soul for You, O God"* (Ps. 42:1). Oh, I like that about David. Too many people are playing church today. They say, "Well, if He comes, fine; if He doesn't, so what." But God is looking for men and women who have a strong, consuming, personal desire to get what they need. Do you want to be healed? Do you want to be delivered? Do you want your home put back together again? Do you want Jesus Christ to come into your life and turn it around? He'll do it if you'll get your desires straight and let Him know about them.

People don't receive their desires because they don't know what they want—or they don't want it bad enough. A lot of the people I pray for come forward in the prayer line and when I ask, "What do you want God to do for you?" they say, "Oh, He knows what I want." He knows, but you don't.

Pastors sometimes help create a wrong attitude in people. When I was a pastor, I fell into the same old rut.

The pastor says, "Now it's time to pray. How many of you have an unspoken request?" And all the hands go up. Every time you go to church, he says, "How many of you have an unspoken request?" It's been the same thing for 10 years.

Do you know why it hasn't been answered? It's unspoken! *"… You do not have because you do not ask"* (James 4:2). Tell Him what you want. Don't hide that thing. God knows what you have need of, but He wants you to desire it. He wants you to ask for it. He said, *"Ask, and it will be given to you; seek, and you will find; knock, and it will be opened to you"* (Matt. 7:7). This is the kind of attitude that God answers.

SIGHT FOR THE BLIND

When I talk about this, the attitude of faith, I can't help but talk about ol' blind Bartimaeus (see Mark 10). Somebody told him, "If a man by the name of Jesus ever comes to town, get to Him. He's a blind man's Healer. I saw Him put clay on another blind man's eyes and then He told him to go wash. When the blind man obeyed, he came back seeing."

Bartimaeus said, "What's His name?"

"Jesus," was the answer.

"Jesus…you're sure now?" Bartimaeus asked.

"That's the Man's name. If He ever comes to town, get to Him!"

Do you realize what that must have done to Bartimaeus's heart and to his praying? I can just hear him, "Oh, come on Jesus, come to my town. I've spent a fortune and still can't see. Please come to my town!"

All of a sudden, here He is. Bartimaeus is by the roadside begging for alms. This is the only activity he knows. As people begin to brush by him, running to the center of town, Bartimaeus says, "Who is it? Who is it? Why is everybody running? Who is it?" He reaches out and grabs hold of a man's coat and says, "Who has come to our town?" The man answers, "A Man by the name of Jesus is passing by."

His attitude isn't, well, I'll sit here and wait until He comes by (just like church folks). No, not Bartimaeus. He pitches his voice in the direction of the noisy crowd and begins to yell, "Hey, Jesus, over here, Man. Have mercy on me."

Oh, that's desire! But Jesus keeps right on walking. It doesn't stop Him. All those people around Bartimaeus start to hush him up, saying, "Hold your peace, man. Here's a quarter—sit back down there and beg." But Bartimaeus throws that tin cup away and yells, "Who do you think's blind around here, man?"

The Bible says he started to shout louder and louder! I can just see him, jumping up and down. "Hey, Jesus, over here! Have mercy on me!"

How bad do you want Jesus' attention? You sit there and play patty-cake in church and say, "Come by here, Lord, come by here." But Bartimaeus jumped up and down, and the Bible says, *Jesus stood still.* He tells His disciples, "Go get him and bring him to Me."

The disciples come running over to Bartimaeus and say, "Be of good cheer. The Lord just called for you. You've been blind for the last day. When you come before Him, you're going to see because of your personal desire!"

CHAPTER 4

The Action of Faith

It's not enough for us to have an initiative and a personal desire. God also demands obedience—personal obedience. This is the action of faith. *Whatever He says to you, do it.*

The most important thing in your life is to be obedient. I'm not talking about being obedient to the rules and regulations of the church. I'm talking about being obedient to whatever "thus saith the Lord" is.

Mary, Jesus' mother, recognized this and said, "Whatever He says to you, you do it, and you'll see a miracle in your life." God demands personal obedience from everyone. If you're willing and obedient, you will enjoy God's blessings.

God is not only concerned about a proper attitude, but also an appropriate action. Look at John 2:7: *"Jesus said to them, 'Fill the waterpots with water.' And they filled them up to the brim."* I call this the action of faith. It's not enough to have the right attitude. You've also got to get up and start putting feet to that thing. Step out on His Word. He's looking for you to take some kind of action.

If you want a miracle, you've got to move on what He says. Jesus said to the servants, "Fill the waterpots with water."

Can't you just hear them saying, "No, Sir, we're not out of water, we're out of wine!" You can get into an argument with God when you need something, but you need to do just what He tells you to do, even if it sounds crazy!

My Jesus, He's a Miracle-Worker, and all He's looking for is a little bit of faith in action. Faith is a fact, but fact is also an act.

Jesus always said, "Rise, take up your bed, and walk." Some of the people He prayed for, He never touched.

When the Lord tells you to do something, He'll give you the ability to do it. Maybe you can't walk, but when the Man of God says, "Rise and walk," get up and take the first step of faith, and God will give you the next 45 steps.

Jesus walked into a synagogue on the Sabbath. (See Mark 3:1-6.) And the Jews wondered, "Is He going to heal on the Sabbath?" He sure put their minds at ease. He walked right up to a man and said, "Hey, you with the withered hand, stand up." The man said, "Yes, Sir." Jesus commanded, "Stretch forth your hand!" Now if He did that today, do you know what folks would say? "Brother Jesus, I've been like this for 20 years." But not that man. When Jesus said, "Stretch forth your hand," that man didn't know any better. He just said, "Yes, Sir."

He stood up, stretched forth his withered hand—right on the Sabbath day. And Jesus healed him because he acted upon the Lord's Word. It's time to act. It's time to say, "Yes, Lord. I believe Your Word." Then you will be the recipient of your miracle. *Whatever He says to you, do it.*

CHAPTER 5

The Affirmation of Faith

Now, God not only looks for our action of faith, but our affirmation of faith. God will always affirm—or confirm— when you act.

When did the water turn into wine? Think about it now. Jesus said, *"Fill the waterpots with water"* (John 2:7). And the Bible says the servants filled those waterpots with water.

They could have sat there all night long and looked at it. Have you ever heard anyone say, "I'm not waiting for the manifestation of it." I hear that today more than any other time in my ministry. Waiting for the affirmation! I'm tired of waiting. I want to see it *now*. When did the miracle happen? That water wasn't turned into wine until He said, "Now draw it out." And when they began to pour it out, it was wine.

HEALING FOR THE SICK

I'm reminded of the story of Naaman the leper. (See Second Kings 5:1-19.) He spent a fortune trying to cure his leprosy, and nobody could cure it. During a battle, this general took a little maid captive and brought her back to wait on his wife. That little maid, cleaning the house one day, said to Naaman's wife, "I wish your husband was back in my hometown. I've got a pastor back there that would lay his hands on him and heal him."

I love that. Here's a woman who had confidence in her pastor. I believe we ought to have confidence in our pastors.

The Bible says, *"Is anyone among you sick?"* The apostle James doesn't say to call the evangelist. He says, *"Let him call for the elders of the church"* (note that it says "elders"—plural) *"…and let them pray over him, anointing him with oil in the name of the Lord. And the prayer of faith will save the sick, and the lord will raise him up. And if he has committed sins, he will be forgiven"* (James 5:14-15).

This woman believed in her pastor. "I wish he was back in my hometown in Samaria. My pastor would help him recover from leprosy."

Now Naaman was a Syrian, a captain in the Syrian army. This army was waging war against God's people. And yet God delivered His own people into Naaman's hand and allowed Naaman to conquer them. Naaman went to the king of Israel first with a letter from the king of Syria, asking the Jewish king to cure Naaman of his leprosy.

The king of Israel said, "Who does he think I am? God? Can I kill and make alive again?" Some of you seeking healing are going to the wrong places. You can't run off to the root and herb doctors to get healed. You can't run off to some dignitary to get healed. You've got to deal with the source of the problem. You've got to come to a man of God to receive the prayer of faith.

Now, Elisha heard that the king had rent his clothes. So the prophet sent his servant, Gehazi, to tell the king that there was a prophet in town. "Tell Naaman to come to the prophet."

Naaman came with his chauffeur-driven chariot, ten changes of raiment, silver, and gold, thinking he could buy his healing. Naaman didn't even go into the prophet's house. He told his servant, "Go get him and tell him to come out."

That's how some folks come to a tent meeting. They want me to set up a booth so they can have drive-through service. They think we have a "McDonald's Revival"! They don't want to sit in church. They want to go see the late show. They want me to sit in a booth with my hand stretched out just so they can go by and touch it and move on.

That's what Naaman wanted the man of God to do. The servant went and knocked on Elisha's door. The prophet didn't even get up; he was in there, sitting in his rocking chair. He said, "Get the door, Gehazi." He knew who it was.

Gehazi went to the door, opened it, and the servant of Naaman said, "The master's here, come out and heal him. Tell the man of God Naaman's out here."

Gehazi went back in and said, "There's a fellow out here by the name of Naaman."

The prophet said, "I know him. And I've got a message for him. Tell him to go jump in the lake. And tell him to do it seven times while he's at it."

"Are you sure you want me to tell him that?" Gehazi asked.

"Yes," the prophet replied. "Tell him what I told you."

Gehazi went back to Naaman's servant and said, "I've got a message for you. The prophet isn't coming out. But he told me to tell your boss to go dip seven times in the Jordan River."

"Do you want me to lose my job?" the servant asked. "I'm not going to tell him to do that."

"Then he isn't going to be healed, because whatever the prophet says to do, he'd better do it."

This is the affirmation of faith. When the man of God tells you to do something, you'd better do it.

The servant went back to that chariot and told Naaman the prophet wasn't coming out to see him. Naaman had traveled a long distance to see Elisha. Now his servant was telling him the prophet didn't want to see him. "I've got a message for you," the servant said to Naaman. "The man of God…well, do you remember that river we just crossed, the Jordan…that ol' muddy thing?"

"Yes," Naaman said.

"Well…" the servant hesitated, "…you're supposed to dip in it seven times."

"You mean to tell me that I've come the whole way from Jordan to dip in that muddy mess?" Naaman screamed. "I'm not going to do it."

Naaman was angry. So his servant spoke very quietly, "Why don't you just humble yourself and do what the man of God tells you to do? You brought silver and gold…you don't have to buy anything. All you have to do is do what he said." *Whatever He says,* **do it!**

Finally Naaman agreed. He went down to that muddy river, took his $500 boots off, and went into the water. I'm sure that old mud started squishing up through his toes…stirring up the water, getting dirtier than ever! *Oh, I hope my friends don't see me! They'll think I've lost my mind,* Naaman thought to himself.

He went down one time; he went down two times; he went down three times, came up out of the water, and said to his servant, "Let's pack up and get out of here. I'm getting this thing infected. Let's go back home. We've got spring water back there."

The servant replied, "No, the man of God said dip seven times. Now get with it! You're already wet; you might as well do it." Naaman went down the fourth time, the fifth, and the sixth.

When he went down the seventh time and came up, he had brand-new baby flesh all over him! He was healed by the power of God! What the doctors couldn't do, God did for him.

THE TESTING OF YOUR FAITH

God is concerned about every one of us. But you've got to do what He tells you to do. God wants to affirm His Word in your life. But I don't care who you are, your faith has to be tested.

Abraham was called the father of all who believe. God gave Isaac to Abraham at 100 years of age. He brought forth a son from his own loins. His wife, Sarah, had a barren womb, but God touched her body, and she gave birth to Isaac.

After that boy began to grow, God said to Abraham, "Get Isaac, and take him up on the mountain and offer him as a sacrifice." If that had been you or me, we would have said it was the devil trying to cheat us out of a blessing.

But Abraham knew the voice of his God. He didn't question Him one time as the sacrificial elements were gathered. He said, "Isaac, we're going up on the mountain to offer a sacrifice to God. Gather the lumber—I've got the knife and the rope to bind the sacrifice." Some of Abraham's servants went with them.

Abraham got halfway up the mountain, and he told his servants to stay behind. "Isaac and I are going up to offer a sacrifice, and we'll be back," he said.

Oh, I like that. "*We'll* be back." I believe there's a thin line between the natural and the supernatural. When did the water turn into wine at the wedding feast in Cana? When did God see faith in Abraham?

Abraham went to the top of that mountain and built an altar. He got Isaac and tied him to it. He pulled his knife out, but God didn't stop him. He raised that knife high above his son. God still didn't stop him. This is the thin line between the natural and the supernatural. The moment he gripped that knife for the downward plunge…God got hold of his arm. He said, "Now I know you love Me more than you love your own son."

You can stay in that sick bed all you want to, but you'll never be well until you take the first step and get up and start walking. Then God will give you your miracle.

Jesus told the servants to fill the waterpots with water and then draw it out. They were putting their reputation on the line. Can you imagine what would have happened if those servants had taken those waterpots filled with water to the master of the feast? They would have been out of a job if it didn't work.

Let's go back to John 2:5: *"Whatever He says to you, do it."* This is how to see a miracle. This is the anatomy of a miracle.

CHAPTER 6

The Achievement of Faith

Now we come to the final principle. After the affirmation of faith, we reach the achievement of faith. All you've got to do is look at verse 10 in that same chapter, and you'll see the accomplishments of faith. *"And he said to him, 'Every man at the beginning sets out the good wine, and when the guests have well drunk, then the inferior. You have kept the good wine until now!' This beginning of signs Jesus did in Cana of Galilee, and manifested His glory; and His disciples believed in Him"* (John 2:10-11).

THE FOUR DIMENSIONS OF FAITH

The achievement of faith is four-dimensional. Four things happened in the achievement of faith in this miracle.

First, *faith always brings God's best.* You show God some faith, and He's going to give you His best. Even the world will know it's God's best. The master of the feast was drinking that wine when he went to the host of the wedding and said, "Why have you kept the best wine until last?" We could say the same thing about the new wine of the Holy Ghost.

In these last days, we're seeing a wave of God's power never before witnessed that will climax the Book of Acts in our day. The Church began in a blaze of His power, and the Church is going to be raptured in a blaze of His power—in a double-portion fashion. God has saved the best wine until the last day. And you and I are a part of it!

Second, *faith blesses others*. Everyone at the wedding was able to drink. I like that. When you put your faith to work it won't just bless you; it'll bless everybody around you.

I was preaching in Peoria, Illinois, and was having lunch in the hotel, getting ready to go and study for the evening service, when five men ganged up on me. They came over and said, "You're Schambach, aren't you?"

I said, "Yes, sir."

One of them said, "We're all Baptist preachers." They pulled up chairs, sat down, and spent four hours with me that afternoon.

They said, "Brother Schambach, we traveled 370 miles to hear you preach tonight. You don't know this, but when we were Baptist students at Southern University in Louisville, Kentucky, we'd sneak out of class to hear you on radio. We'd get in an automobile and turn your program on. We loved to hear you preach.

"One day you said, 'I dare you Baptists to lay your hands on the radio.' We were determined that no Pentecostal preacher was going to dare us to do anything. All five of us put our hands on the dashboard of that car, and all five of us started talking in another language. God filled us with the Holy Ghost and fire!"

Out of your belly shall flow *rivers* of living water. In this last day, we're going to see a revival of the outpouring of the Holy Ghost like you've never seen before. You might as well get Him now and not wait until then. You're a candidate to receive.

Faith brings God's best—that's the first dimension. Faith blesses others—that's the second dimension.

The third dimension of faith is—faith begets faith. Are you listening to me? Doubt begets—or breeds—doubt. Fear begets fear. When you are afraid, you'll make someone else afraid. When you doubt, somebody else will doubt. But when you have faith, you'll help somebody else have faith.

Because Jesus performed this miracle, His disciples believed on Him. Up until this point, they didn't—they just followed Him. But because of what their eyes saw, a demonstration of the miraculous and the supernatural, and because of the faith of Jesus, all the disciples believed on Him. When you have faith, somebody else is going to have faith.

The fourth dimension of faith is—faith glorifies God. Without faith it is impossible to please God. When you learn how to trust God, you are glorifying Him.

Do you want to glorify God? Then get rid of your sickness. Get rid of your disease. Get rid of your sin. Receive the Holy Ghost. Lay claim to every promise in the Bible, and you will glorify God by saying, "Lord, I believe Your Word. I lay claim on it now. It belongs to me. I claim it for myself and claim it for my family."

When you learn how to put faith to work, you will receive a miracle in your life. Do you want a miracle? Do you want God to save you? Do you want to be healed? Do you want God to deliver you and set you free? Do you want Him to fill you with the Holy Ghost? You don't have to wait until tomorrow. You can get your miracle right now because Jesus is with you right now. You can receive your miracle!

Let me pray for you:

Dear Jesus, I come to You on behalf of this friend who needs a miracle. Lord, I release Your miracle power in this friend's life today! We're obeying Your Word and doing what You said to do. Your Word says to cast all our care on You because You care for us. So we're bringing this miracle need to You in faith, believing.

Lord, You see this need. You understand this problem. You know all about this situation. As we come to You, heal this body...restore this family...forgive every fault and failure...strengthen every weakness...provide abundance for every lack and need. Take what we have and miraculously turn it into what we need—just as You turned the water into wine.

Oh God, we love You. We appreciate You and thank You in advance for Your miracle power that is already moving in our behalf. Bless this friend now in a special way, and we'll be careful to give You the praise and the glory and the honor forever, Amen.

PART II

Miracles of SALVATION

and DELIVERANCE

The Greatest Miracle

Praise God! I never get tired of talking about miracles. I have seen so many amazing miracles throughout my years of preaching the Gospel. But still, the greatest miracle by far is when God reaches down, takes out a stony heart, and puts in a heart of flesh—when He takes a filthy sinner, clothes him with the righteousness of God, and writes his name in the Lamb's Book of Life. There is no greater miracle.

That is what God wants to do for every person on the face of the earth. When He revealed His promised Deliverer, Jesus Christ, He provided a way for everyone to receive this miracle.

In the city of Nazareth, at the beginning of Jesus' early ministry, He stood up in the temple one day to read a very significant Scripture that revealed His heart for a ministry and outlined the earthly mission His Father had given Him:

The Spirit of the Lord is upon Me, because He has anointed Me to preach the gospel to the poor; He has sent Me to heal the brokenhearted, to proclaim liberty to the captives and recovery of sight to the blind, to set at liberty those who are oppressed; to proclaim the acceptable year of the Lord (Luke 4:18-19).

Jesus was quoting from the book of Isaiah. As He read, a synagogue filled with religious people noticed something different about this young rabbi. The words were not simply being recited; they were being adopted as a personal creed. Jesus was revealing Himself as the fulfillment of this specific prophecy.

Now anyone enslaved by sin, oppressed by the devil, owned by corruption and evil, could make a clean break from their old lives and start over by accepting Jesus Christ as Deliverer and Savior. No matter how much of a sinner a person may be, God has a great miracle of deliverance waiting for him or her.

In the next few pages you will read some outstanding testimonies of deliverance I have witnessed. Just remember, when Christ comes into the heart of an individual, when all things become new, that person has received the greatest miracle!

Chapter 7

Prizefighter Goes Down for the Count

When I was pastoring in Newark, New Jersey, there was a dear woman in our church named Sister Price. She came to me one night about her husband. He was an old "boozer." All he did was drink. No matter how hard she tried, she could never get him to come to church with her.

She said, "Brother Schambach, you don't know what kind of devil I married. I've done everything for him, but he won't come to church with me. I've tried everything. I'm tired of it!"

"Well, I'm glad you're tired of it," I told her.

"You mean I can leave him?"

"Oh no, girl," I said. "You picked him out all by yourself. You said you're tired of it? Good. Now we're going to put it in God's hands."

So I laid hands on her and said, "Holy Ghost, sic him! Knock him down and drag him to the foot of the cross!"

I was running a revival there in Newark, so we had a service the next night. During the meeting, this big guy came in. He was about six-feet-two, 270 pounds. Solid steel! And he came walking up that center aisle like he owned the place.

I jumped off that platform and headed down toward him. I was walking like I owned the place. I met him face to face, head-on, jaw to jaw—an irresistible force meeting an immovable object.

"Are you the preacher?"

"Yes, sir," I said. "I'm the man of God here."

"They tell me you can help me."

"You smell like you need help, brother."

Then he said sarcastically, "You want to help me? Buy me a fifth of liquor!"

I felt my fist doubling up. The old Schambach was coming alive, the one who's supposed to be crucified with Christ. Do you know what I'm talking about? I wanted to give him a knuckle sandwich right there! But my hand went limp. The Holy Ghost wouldn't allow me to hit him. And boy, am I glad! I found out later that he was an all-state boxing champ!

So I went to lay hands on him, but the Holy Ghost wouldn't even let me touch him. I got about two inches from him and he just fell back—*bam*! He hit solid concrete!

Then Sister Price ran out shouting, "Aaahh! Glory! That's that devil I'm married to!"

I said, "Hush, woman. Don't say any more. He's here now. Let the Holy Ghost do His job now." So he lay there on that floor.

When he got up, he was sober and ready to receive Christ as his Savior. God saved him and filled him with the Holy Ghost and fire. He was speaking in other tongues and praising God!

God worked a miracle! He made a lamb out of a lion. After that, Brother Price preached the Gospel for many years in New York, New Jersey, Virginia, North Carolina, and all over the East Coast. He went on home to be with the Lord, but his wife, dear Sister Georgia Price, continued singing and telling the story of how God made her violent old husband a new creature through the delivering power of Jesus Christ.

CHAPTER 8

From Junk to Jesus

I have many friends who have helped partner with my ministry over the years. A lot of them have great stories of what God has done for them through my ministry. I'll never forget the story of a certain partner of mine, Brother James Wallace, another "lost cause" who was transformed by the power of Christ.

In August of 1975 I had my tent up in the Bronx, New York. Many preachers are afraid to go into the ghetto—into places like the Bronx. But I love to take the Gospel where it is needed! I love to take it right into the heart of the inner city. To see God perform miracles and deliver those who are bound by the devil. You see, a lot of these folks won't set foot in a church. So I bring church to them. People who wouldn't go into a church come pouring into my tent meetings, and that's when God takes over!

Now, James Wallace was just that kind of person. He was raised in one of the most hellish neighborhoods of the Bronx. At an early age he had experimented with many different types of pills and drugs, and as a teenager he became an alcoholic.

Circumstances from his environment and his own young rebellion filled him with a violent rage. He broke the law often and found himself in and out of police precincts and jail. James adopted the attitudes of his environment—he trusted no one but himself. Eventually he became a racist, hating all white people.

In his early twenties, James was living with his girlfriend, not wanting to marry her because he knew he would be a high-risk father in many ways. Life went from bad to worse when the doctors told him he had cirrhosis of the liver. James needed help.

In the eyes of man, he was not a likely candidate for salvation. But what is impossible with man is possible with God!

One day James pulled up in his car to 149th Street and the Major Deegan Expressway in the Bronx. He was parked in front of a Gospel tent that was as big as a football field. It looked like a circus tent. All he could hear was the voice of a preacher who was shouting about something.

James felt anger rising up within him. The preacher was a white man, and as far as he could tell, he was preaching about a white God named Jesus. Against his better judgment, James went inside to see what was happening.

That preacher was me, and I was telling people that Jesus could free them from sin, heal their bodies, and deliver them from addictions.

Then, I asked some people from the vast audience to come forward and tell others what Jesus had done for them. James heard stories of deaf ears opening, drug addicts being instantly set free, and people being healed from cancer. One thread of every story was the same—each of the storytellers said Jesus had done the work in their lives. At first, James refused to believe what he was hearing. He thought all preachers were either pimps or sissies. Yet, James could not deny there was something powerful and real happening under that tent.

Night after night he would come back to listen. Then one night James mustered up the courage to go forward and let the preacher pray for him.

When I prayed for him, James said a prayer, "God, if You're real, let me feel something."

James didn't feel anything right away. In his mind he was saying, "See, I knew this thing was fake. Nothing happened."

He went right across the street to the bar and ordered some drinks.

But that night he realized something. He had lost his taste and needs for alcohol. He had no more shakes. He had no withdrawal symptoms. He was free from alcohol, and he knew it.

The next night, James went back to the tent. He knelt at an altar and asked Jesus Christ to forgive him. When James got off his knees, he was delivered from his addictions and healed of cirrhosis of the liver. Today, he is married, has four children, and is pastoring a church in the Bronx.

James is still partnering with my ministry today. He serves as a testimony of the power of God to set the captives free! In his own words:

"Jesus is the answer. He has set me free from pushing dope to preaching hope. From crime to Christ. From junk to Jesus."

CHAPTER 9

Man Spared From Electric Chair

This is one of the greatest miracles I have ever witnessed. I was preaching in Newark, New Jersey, in 1960. It is so vivid, I remember the time: 9:30. A woman came walking down the center aisle. I knew what that meant. It meant, "I am going to disturb you, preacher." She walked down that center aisle and stood right in front of me. I had my Bible in my hand, and I was preaching—I was preaching a masterpiece! She interrupted me. How dare anybody interrupt a man of God?

Actually, I would hope more preachers were interrupted by someone with faith. Four men stopped Jesus when they tore the roof off and lowered down a man on a cot. They stopped Him from preaching. Remember what happened to the man on the cot?

When that woman came down and stopped me, she said, "Brother Schambach, please forgive me. I have never stopped a preacher in my life. But this is an emergency. My son is going to die in the electric chair at ten o'clock."

I said, "Oh, my God!" She knocked the preacher right out of me. I couldn't preach another word.

I had prayed for people dying in hospitals, but I had never prayed for anybody who was going to die in the electric chair. This man had been convicted by a jury of his peers. He had been found guilty. He was going to die in order to pay for the murder that they said he committed—and it was going to happen in 30 minutes. I couldn't preach! I shut the book. I couldn't even pray! I had everybody in the church stand.

People ask me, "Do I need the Holy Ghost?" I don't know about you, but I do. Sometimes I don't know how to pray. When I don't know how to pray, I let the Holy Ghost do the praying.

The Holy Ghost began to pray through me. I felt like somebody just put a robe on me. I could feel the anointing. A double portion came on me. I was praying in tongues. I wanted to eavesdrop on what the Holy Ghost was saying. How can you eavesdrop? Pray in English. So I stopped. When you are praying in the Spirit, your understanding is unfruitful. I didn't know what I was saying. Then all of a sudden, the understanding began to speak, and the spirit was unfruitful. I began to pray in English, and what I was saying shocked me.

I will never forget my prayer. I was saying, "Lord, in the name of Jesus, convict the real killer through the Holy Ghost. Make him confess to the crime." Inside, I was kicking myself. I thought, "Shut up, dummy. The man has already been convicted." I was asking God to get a hold of the real killer. I didn't know, but the Holy Ghost knew that this woman's son hadn't committed the crime. The Holy Ghost was praying through me and saying, "Get a hold of the real killer and make him confess."

After I finished praying, I looked at that woman and said, "Go home, go to bed—and sleep! Your son will not die in the electric chair!" I could have kicked myself. I thought, *Shut up, you dumb preacher! Remember, you have to come back here tomorrow night and preach!*

Sometimes the Holy Ghost will say things that are difficult for you to believe. Sometimes when you are preaching, you say things that startle you. But it isn't you talking, it is the Holy Ghost.

Are you ready for the outcome of this story?

I returned to my hotel and went to bed. I got up the next morning and went to the diner a block away. On my way in, I bought the *New York Daily News*. Glory! Did you ever shout looking at a newspaper? Well, I did. You know what the headlines said? "Man's Life Spared from Electric Chair—Story on page 3." I didn't eat breakfast. Oh, no. I sat down on that curb and tore open the paper to page three. I can tell you what that newspaper said verbatim. I can tell you the name of the district attorney. His name was Mr. Hogan. The story said, "Last night at 9:40, Mr. Hogan received a phone call from a man." (Remember, it was 9:30 when the woman disturbed me. At 9:40, God answered the woman's prayer. Oh, hallelujah!) The man on the other end said, "You are burning the wrong man."

"What do you mean? Who is this?" asked Mr. Hogan.

"Nevermind who it is. But you have a man scheduled to die in the electric chair for the murder of a man in the upper Bronx. You found his body in a second-floor apartment, face down with stab wounds."

Mr. Hogan said, "How do you know this?"

He said, "I am the one who committed the crime."

"Where are you?" Mr. Hogan asked.

He answered, "I am two blocks from a certain precinct. And I am on my way in to give myself up."

Mr. Hogan stopped the execution. He went to the precinct and interrogated the new suspect until three o'clock in the morning, going over the same question. "Why did you give yourself up?"

Repeatedly the same answer came, "Man, I never had any intentions of giving myself up. But when I called you last night, something got a hold of me and made me confess."

CHAPTER 10

It's Never Too Late

Some time ago, when I was in Seattle, Washington, I preached a message about Lazarus. The Bible says that Lazarus had been in the grave four days when Jesus finally came. Although it seemed as if He had arrived too late, He was right on time. He is never too late. In other words, it's never too late for a miracle.

Sometimes we put time limits on God. Mary and Martha were limited in their faith. They said to Jesus, *"Lord, if You had been here, my brother would not have died"* (John 11:21,32). They had forgotten that Jesus was Christ, the Son of God—Emmanuel: God with us. They had forgotten that Jesus is the Resurrection and the Life.

They didn't know that Jesus had intentionally waited. He wanted His followers to witness His miraculous power.

We should never try to figure out God's timetables. He is always on time. It's never too late.

After the service, a woman came to me and shoved a piece of paper into my hand. She said, "Now, I dare you to say it's not too late." Do you know what the paper was? A divorce paper, a final decree. She had just received it from the judge. It was final. The husband was gone. She looked me right in the eye and said again, "Now, I dare you to say it's not too late."

So I smiled and took her dare and said, "It's not too late."

She said, "What about that paper?"

I said, "You are looking at the wrong paper. My paper says, *'Therefore what God has joined together, let not man separate'* (Matt. 19:6). That is what I believe. How long have you been married?" She told me they had been married for 27 years and had five children. I said, "That man has no business leaving you." I laid hands on her and said, "Holy Ghost, bring that rascal to his senses and save him. Don't bring him back home the way he is. Lord, save him and fill him with the Holy Ghost." I looked at the woman and said, "Go home and get ready for your husband. He is coming."

Of course, that was easy for me to say. I was leaving town. I am an evangelist. I can hit them and run. But in all honesty, I believed what I had said. My wife and I drove from Seattle to Philadelphia. When we got to Philly, I had a letter, from that woman, waiting for me. I opened it, and the first lines said, "Dear Brother Schambach, God is never too late! God got a hold of that rascal, saved him, and filled him with the Holy Ghost. The Lord brought him back home, and we got married all over again."

That is the powerful aspect of faith. Take a stand of faith and say, "Devil, you are a liar. I am going to believe God for a miracle because He is going to turn this situation around." Speak faith. Speak to that mountain, and that mountain has to obey your words. That is how you will experience the power of faith.

CHAPTER 11

I Died Last Night

I'll never forget one of the most unusual things that happened under the tent. It was during one of the greatest revivals I have ever had—and a man died in the fourth row.

Immediately I went to him with my Bible. I wasn't going to let the devil kill anybody in my meeting. I commanded the devil to turn him loose. I called his spirit back into his body. There were no signs of life. I told my tent crew, "Come and take him behind the platform. No one is going to disturb my preaching." They took him there. Somehow we actually forgot about him.

The next night I returned to the tent. During the meeting I asked, "I want five of the happiest people here tonight to come up and tell us what you are happy about."

The dead man was first in line!

I didn't recognize him. He was dressed up. I handed him the microphone and asked, "What are you happy about, brother?"

"Praise God!" he replied. "I died last night."

I thought, *What kind of nut do I have here?*

But he looked at me in a strange way and said, "Don't you remember me?"

"No sir," I replied. "I don't remember you."

"You walked through four rows of chairs to get to me," he answered. "Brother Schambach, I had my fifth heart attack in your tent last night. Doctors told me if I had one more heart attack, it would kill me. My body was there, but my spirit was gone. I saw you running back through those people. You called my spirit back into my body." Tears started running down his face. "I am so thankful you did that," he said, "because last night I was a sinner and I would have gone to hell if you hadn't stopped my spirit. My spirit came back into my body. I woke up behind that platform with a brand-new heart. I got saved and filled with the Holy Ghost last night. I went to my doctor today, and he couldn't believe it."

The man shouted, "Jesus came into my heart last night and gave me a brand new heart. Hallelujah!"

His doctor had said to him, "Where are the other four scars on your heart?" He couldn't find the scars from the previous attacks. "You have the heart of a 25-year-old man."

Since that night, when God directs me, I don't hesitate to lay hands on any dead folks because they may not be saved. I would like them to be saved—saved from the burning flames of hell! That man was on his way to hell, but thank God, I got a hold of that spirit before the devil could claim him. God saved him and filled him with the Holy Ghost and with fire.

CHAPTER 12

The First Devil I Ever Cast Out

I will never forget the first devil I cast out. I was with Brother A. A. Allen in Los Angeles. He cast the devils out of a girl who came to our meeting. We then moved to Phoenix, and when I saw her walk inside the tent, I said, "Oh, Lord, they are all back, plus another thousand."

When Brother Allen saw her, he said, "Do you see what I see?"

I said, "Yes, sir."

"Oh," he said, "I can't tackle them tonight. If I pray for the sick, I won't be able to deliver her also. Take her in the prayer tent and cast them out."

I said, "What? You are the preacher."

He said, "I won't have anybody working with me who doesn't know how to cast out devils."

This was "where the rubber met the road." This was the "nitty gritty" now. This wasn't just playing church. I went to the platform and asked 12 of the pastors to come with me.

They said, "Where are we going?"

I said, "To battle. We are going to the prayer tent to battle." I picked six women with husky voices. I said, "Get the Blood songs ready. Just sing Blood songs. We are going to conquer the devil."

I was there from ten o'clock at night until one o'clock in the morning wrestling with those demons. I wrestled with the devils. It felt as though I had lost 30 pounds casting those demons out.

For we do not wrestle against flesh and blood, but against principalities, against powers, against the rulers of the darkness of this age, against spiritual hosts of wickedness in the heavenly places (Ephesians 6:12).

I said, "Devil, in the name of Jesus, you are coming out."

The devil answered me back and said, "We are not coming out."

It wasn't just, "I am not" but "We are not."

I wanted to say, "Go ahead, fella, stay where you are. I am not going to bother you."

But we ganged up on them. I quoted every Scripture passage I knew. I found out you can't beat the air and pound them out. You can't stomp them out. You can't knock them out. You can't Scripture-quote them out. You have to cast them out. This is what God told us to do. Finally, at three o'clock in the morning, the devil said, "We are going to wear you out."

He didn't know how close to the truth he was. I said, "Devil, we don't wear out." I felt like somebody put a mantle on me. I said, "Satan, my elder brother Jesus destroyed you 2,000 years ago." The moment I said, the voice inside that woman said, "Don't say that."

I said, "I got him. I got him!" So, being an obedient servant, I shouted it again. I learned my lesson a long time ago. When the devil tells you not to do something, do it. And when he tells you to do something, you don't do it.

I said, "He has his bags packed. He is on his way." I shouted it louder one more time.

The devil said, "I know it. But don't say it so loud. Everybody doesn't know it."

When Jesus died on Calvary and shed His blood, He paid the price. I believe the devils came out of everybody so they could gather around the cross of Calvary and wring their hands and say, "We got Him now."

But they didn't have Him! Jesus died on the cross, defeating sin and Satan. No one destroyed the kingdom of the devil like Jesus did!

I am He who lives, and was dead, and behold, I am alive forevermore. Amen. And I have the keys of Hades and of Death (Revelation 1:18).

Those devils finally came out of that woman. I made sure that she received Christ into her heart and was baptized in the Holy Ghost. When we heard her speaking in other tongues, we knew those devils would never return again. Praise God!

You are of God, little children, and have overcome them, because He who is in you is greater than he who is in the world (1 John 4:4).

CHAPTER 13

Broken Needles and a Phone Call

You can stand in faith for loved ones, believing that God will save them and deliver them. This is what I call "proxy." When two or more are uniting their faith in perfect agreement, God will perform a miracle. I want to share two stories with you about people who stood proxy for their loved ones.

Back in the 1960s, I rented a synagogue in Philadelphia, and I held a revival there for two weeks. While I was there, an elderly woman came to see me about her son, who was hooked on drugs. She said, "He has come into the house and stolen every light. He stole the couch. He stole the rugs. My house is bare! He took it all and sold it to pump into his arm!"

When you're hooked on drugs, you're going to find it somewhere. Every one of you who used to be a drug addict (or still are one) knows what I'm talking about. You'll find it somewhere.

She said, "I can't get him to church."

"He doesn't have to come to church," I told her. Then I laid hands on her and prayed the same prayer that I prayed for Brother Price in Newark. "Holy Ghost, sic him!"

After I prayed, the Lord gave me a prophetic word for the woman. "Go on home. Your son is delivered."

You might say, "Well, anyone could have said that to her." But I was operating under the anointing of the Holy Ghost. He doesn't lie! So I knew that her son was delivered.

I came back to the synagogue the next night. The same little lady had come back to the service. This time she had a young man with her. She got my attention. This young man had a story to tell. There's always a story to tell. Hallelujah!

The night before he had been in an alley with a needle, trying to give himself a shot, when the needle broke. But drug addicts are used to that. They always carry a spare in their billfold. So he pulled the spare out and tried to inject it into his arm. Then that needle broke!

He had to have a quick fix, so he went to his pusher's apartment. (Now, from what I'm told, that's a no-no!)

He beat on the door. The guy opened the door.

"What are you doing at my house?" he said. "Get in here!"

"Man, I need a quick fix," the young man told him. "I got the drugs from you earlier, but I broke two needles. Get me a needle. I need a shot now."

So the pusher went to get him another needle.

What this young man told me next thrilled me. Right there in the pusher's apartment, something left him. He suddenly had no cravings for the drug. Right there in front of the pusher, a miracle took place!

The pusher tried to force it on him. "Here's the needle. Give yourself—"

"No, wait. I don't need it. Something happened; I don't know what it was."

Then he gave the drugs back that he had bought earlier. Now, this is another no-no to the drug addict. But he was delivered! He was set free! He didn't need them anymore.

That night, his mama was coming home from church. If you've ever been to our meetings, you know we keep them a little lengthy. She was getting back to her house around midnight. To her surprise, her son showed up. This was early for him. He never came in before two, three, or four o'clock in the morning. (It didn't matter. He didn't have a bed anyway. He had stolen it and sold it already.)

When his mama saw him coming up those steps, she said, "What are you doing home so early?"

He said, "Mother, I don't know. Something happened to me tonight." And he told her the story I told you.

"Oh!" she said. "Brother Schambach laid hands on me and sent the Word to you and commanded that devil to turn you loose. That monkey is off of your back right now!"

Oh, hallelujah! He was in the service that night and got saved, sanctified, and filled with the Holy Ghost.

There was another lady who came to me one time. She said, "Oh, Brother Schambach. I have a daughter who ran away from home, and I don't know where she is. I haven't heard from her for six years."

And I said, "God will do it." Then I prayed that same prayer. "Holy Ghost, sic her! Knock her down where she is! Bring her to the foot of the cross. And tonight, make her dial her mother's phone number."

When I got done, I looked at that woman and said, "Go home and sit by the phone. You're going to get a call from your daughter."

She came back the next night shouting and jumping. She had a great testimony. She said, "Brother Schambach, it was just like you said. When I got home, I sat by the phone. My daughter called me for the first time in six years. She said, 'I don't know why I'm calling you, but something got a hold of me.' I said, 'That's the Holy Ghost!'"

This is proxy! You can believe for somebody else. God knows what to do. If He can find two of us here on earth agreeing, as touching anything, that they shall ask and it shall be done.

Are you ready to see that loved one set free? Well, you're going to put your faith to work. You're going to stand proxy for him or her, and God's going to give you the miracle that you've been praying for. Let's pray, shall we?

Father, in the name of Jesus, we ask that You touch the life of these lost loved ones right now. Put a hook in their jaw and drag them to the foot of Calvary. Arrest them in their tracks. Get a hold of them, in Jesus' name. Save them and fill them with the Holy Ghost. We thank You for Your miracle-working power. We ask this in the name of Jesus. Amen and amen.

CHAPTER 14

Voice of Power

I love ministering to people through radio broadcasts. I've been on radio for many years now. There's just something about it. You see, when people hear a broadcast, they can't sit back and judge the preacher because of the way he looks or acts. They can't sit back and say, "Well, I don't like his tie. I don't like his suit. I don't like him!"

They can only judge a preacher by what he says. So when I preach on radio, people can only judge me by the Word of God that I bring forth, not by how I dress or what color I am. In fact, many people think I'm a black preacher!

God has saved and delivered so many people through the "Voice of Power" broadcast. I have three testimonies that I want to share of people who were at the end of their ropes—at the point of suicide—when they heard an old-fashioned Holy Ghost preacher on their radio. God delivered them.

There was a gentleman in Boston who seemed like he had it all. He was a successful businessman. He had a new house, a new car, and a fine family. But he had one downfall—he was an alcoholic.

This tore his family apart. It cost him his job, and eventually his family left him.

"I couldn't afford milk for my baby," he later testified, "but I still bought the booze."

He soon lost his house, too. The last day he was there, he sat alone in that empty house (the furniture was already gone). He figured that he might as well end it all there. He planned to commit suicide.

He turned up the radio as loud as it would go so his neighbors wouldn't hear the gun go off when he shot himself. Just as he was about to pull the trigger, he heard a voice on the radio. It was the voice of a loud, Pentecostal preacher who singled him out.

"Don't touch that dial! Suicide is not your answer! Put your hand on the radio right now, and I'll pray for that spirit of oppression and suicide to leave you."

Immediately, he went to his radio, cradled it in his arms, and prayed that prayer with me. Right there in that empty house, he gave his life to Christ and was instantly delivered from alcoholism.

He got his family back and found an even better job than the one he had lost. In just two years, he was able to pay for a new home as well.

Another man that God delivered through radio was a brother named Montgomery, who had been a pastor. After his church split, he had left the ministry and went into construction.

His church wasn't the only thing that split. He and his wife went through a divorce. His life was falling apart piece by piece.

One morning, a spirit of oppression swept over him, urging him to commit suicide. He tried to stand up against it, but nothing worked. He wanted to kill himself.

That night, he fell into bed and cried out, "God, I put myself in Your care."

God answered him, "Son, I'm sending a prophet." Of course, John had no idea what that meant. At three o'clock in the morning, he turned on the radio in desperation. The "Voice of Power" broadcast was on. At the end of the message, he heard the same kind of charge that the man from Boston had heard.

"Don't turn your radio off. I'm going to pray for someone very specifically…that young preacher who has been tormented by a spirit of suicide today. You foul spirit, I curse you in the name of the Lord Jesus." As soon as I spoke those words, the oppression left instantly and never returned.

The final story is one that came across my desk many years ago from Canada.

There was a family of two parents and three daughters. They were facing a crisis time financially; no one in the household was able to find a job to meet their needs. They literally could not put food on the table.

A heavy depression settled in on the father and spread to the entire family. He and his wife decided it would be better if they all died together, right now, instead of waiting for starvation. So the family formed a suicide pact. They planned to end it all in their garage, inhaling the carbon monoxide fumes.

When the day arrived, they took their places in the car. The father started the car up, but then the mother reached across and shut off the ignition.

"What if we wait just one more day?" she pleaded.

Angrily, the father jumped out of the car. If his wife persisted, he would lose his nerve. He hoped he would be able to get back in the car tomorrow.

In his anger, he went in the house and started kicking things around. Finally, he turned on the radio. The radio man was new to him, but what the preacher was saying captured his attention. The preacher was talking about a demon of suicide that convinces people there's no hope. "Mister, suicide is not the answer to your problems. Jesus Christ is the only answer."

This was the first time the father had heard about Jesus, who not only could save a life from sin, but was able to deliver from all kinds of oppression, including thoughts of suicide.

The entire family realized that tormenting spirit was trying to destroy their lives and send them to hell. On their knees in the living room, an entire family repented of their sins and received Jesus as Lord of their home. Within days, God turned their situation around.

CHAPTER 15

Anointing Oil Ends Demonic Nightmare

God works miracles in many different ways. He uses many different vehicles to display His power in the lives of people. After all, He is a creative God.

One of these is anointing oil. The Bible teaches that oil is to be used to anoint for needs in the name of our Lord (see James 5:14). Now, the oil has no special power in itself, but God often works miracles through its use by the believer. I have seen this many times.

I have anointed many people and have seen God do miraculous things because of it. Then sometimes I distribute oil to other believers so that they can anoint others. I send out many bottles of oil absolutely free to those who request it for needs in their life.

I had a woman and her husband write to my ministry once, requesting the anointing oil for Rosemary, the woman's mother.

For seven months, Rosemary had been demon-possessed. She couldn't eat or drink. Under the evil influence, she broke all the windows in her house and rolled around on the floor. Three grown men could not hold her down! The demons inside her would howl!

She was placed in a mental institution, where she stayed six months. All that time, her daughter and son-in-law prayed for her. Day and night they prayed. It was during this time that they had written to me requesting the oil. They anointed Rosemary and prayed for her deliverance.

Well, some time later, Rosemary herself came back to one of my meetings to testify. She was free! She told the story of how her daughter had anointed her and prayed for her. She was delivered by the power of God! She steadily began to get better, and her physical body was restored as well.

This blesses me! Jesus Christ is still at work today, setting the captives free just like he was 2,000 years ago. He's just looking for people that know how to believe His Word and stand on His promises. When we are obedient to His voice, He can work miracles through us.

Chapter 16

Second Chance

In my meetings, before I preach, I like to have people come to the platform and testify about what God has done in their lives. I love doing this because when people in the audience hear these powerful testimonies, faith begins to stir in their hearts, and then they are ready to receive their own miracle from God.

One night, while I had my tent up in Coney Island, New York, a woman named Lucy came up to the platform with a story to tell.

When she was 13 years of age, she became a lesbian. She started dressing like a man and acting like a man. The devil even had her believing that she was a man. Soon she began using drugs. She hated this lifestyle, but she could not break free. Everything seemed hopeless. She even tried to commit suicide twice. But she failed at that, too.

After 24 years of this torture, she developed herpes.

Once again, in man's eyes, there was no hope for Lucy. It seemed like the end—like it was too late for anything to help her. But it's never too late for Jesus! Hallelujah! He's always right on time!

Maybe your situation seems hopeless. Maybe everybody else has given up on you. I don't care whether you're a drug addict, a homosexual, a lesbian, or on your deathbed with some type of infirmity, Jesus Christ is your cure. It's never too late for Him to perform a miracle!

But back to Lucy. Here she was, sick and dying in her sin. She stood in her bathroom, shaking and scared to death. She didn't want to die. She knew she would go to hell. But in this moment of desperation, she heard a voice. It was the voice of God!

"This is your last chance I am giving you," the voice said to her.

So there in the bathroom, Lucy cried out to God. "Lord, I just want to serve You. Change me, because I don't want to be like this anymore!"

Instantly, she was free. Every bit of demonic oppression left her. The sickness departed from her body. God restored her mind and her womanhood. He saved her and set her feet on the right path. When she told us the story under the tent she was feeling great.

That's the kind of God I serve! He gives us a second chance. If He didn't, this old preacher would have been dead a long time ago. But I'm so glad that He's in the business of restoring people who seem hopeless to everybody else.

CHAPTER 17

Modern-day Jonah

When I was preaching in Canada one year, I had another brother come up to the platform to testify—Pastor Paul Deacock. I tell you folks, I was so glad to hear this story because sometimes as a preacher you wonder, "Is anybody listening out there?" Just to hear a testimony like his makes me want to shout. Let me tell you what happened.

This young man was a former drug dealer in Winnipeg. He had been hooked on crack and all sorts of other drugs. He would go out on binges and get stoned out of his mind. He did all this because he was running from God.

You see, at the age of three, God had called Paul to preach. Although he remembered that very clearly, he continued to run from the call on his life. He didn't want to have anything to do with God.

Yet, he could not get away from the conviction of the Holy Spirit, Who kept telling him God had something better for him.

So he tried to drown out that voice with drugs.

He ended up bed-ridden in his parents' basement for three months. He was miserable and didn't want to live anymore. So in that basement, he cried out, "God, if You're real, come into my life. If not, I'll just kill myself! I have nothing to live for!"

Instantly, God took away his craving for drugs. Oh, I love this—instantly! Listen to me: if God could save this young man, he can save anybody!

God was not done with him yet. After all, He'd called him to preach. When God calls you to do something, He means business!

So in that basement of his parents' house, Paul started reading the Bible from cover to cover. He was so hungry for more of God that he started digging through boxes there in the basement, where he found three sermon LPs by an old-fashioned Holy Ghost preacher named Schambach. These sermons had been spiritual food for his parents when they were seeking the Lord.

He listened to them over and over again. They gave him a foundation in his knowledge of God's Word. He heard about healing the sick, casting out devils, and bringing lost souls to Christ.

Now Paul is a pastor in North Carolina and has his own miracle ministry. He told me that people are being healed of polio, healed of cancer, and that cataracts are disappearing! He has been to nine countries, preaching the Gospel of Christ, and has led hundreds to the Lord.

He came all the way from North Carolina to one of my meetings up in Canada just to shake my hand and let me know what the Lord has done. Hallelujah!

I'll tell you, when God calls somebody, He knows what He's doing! He knows the work that He has in mind for them to accomplish. I'm so glad that my sermons were able to help this man grow in his walk with the Lord.

You know, those same old sermons that I used to preach, the ones he heard in the basement, I'm still preaching them today! Some people get onto me about that. They say, "Brother Schambach, you're still preaching the same thing that you did 20 years ago."

You know what I tell them? I say, "Thank you. You just paid me the greatest compliment!"

God's Word does not change! Hallelujah! I'm not changing my message for anybody! I'm going to keep preaching that same Gospel of power until the Lord takes me home.

CHAPTER 18

Walking the Streets of South Philly

The Bible says, "*God has not given us a spirit of fear…*" (2 Tim. 1:7). It also says, "*…fear involves torment…*" (1 John 4:18). Therefore, I can conclude that fear is a tormenting spirit. Many of God's people are bound by this tormenting spirit of fear, even when they hear the Word preached.

Fear is the opposite of faith. It can keep you from being active as a Christian. If you are bound with a spirit of fear, I don't have to tell you—you need a miracle of deliverance. And I have good news— God wants you to be rid of fear in your life and is ready and willing to set you free.

Once, when I was in Philadelphia, I met a woman who had a problem with fear.

I used to conduct private interviews where people could come and meet with me one on one. This lady came in trying to make an impression. She talked in tongues a little and then sat down.

I said, "What can I do for you?"

She said, "I've come for you to pray for me."

I said, "I don't pray in the daytime. I pray at night. You see, we preach in the daytime to stir your faith. Then we lay hands on you during the night service when faith is alive."

She said, "Well, I can't come at night."

I said, "Are you working?"

"No."

"Do you have an appointment?"

"No."

"Then come back tonight," I told her.

"I'm not coming back."

I said, "Well, I'm not praying."

That might seem harsh, but I knew she was hiding something from me. I discerned it in my own spirit. So I asked her, "What's your problem? I want to know."

She said, "Well, I've got high blood pressure, and I've got sugar diabetes."

"Is that all?" I said.

"Yes, it is," she replied.

I said, "No, you're telling me a lie. You're telling me you can't come tonight. The reason why you can't come is be cause you're bound with a spirit of fear."

She said, "How did you know?"

Listen, she was a child of God. She loved the Lord. But she was still bound by that spirit of fear.

She said, "I haven't been out of my house at night for the last 12 years. Oh, Brother Schambach, this spirit torments me."

I said, "Look, stay until tonight. Go next door and buy a sandwich. Stay here, and I'll pray for you tonight. I'll get rid of that spirit of fear. God's given me the power to cast out devils, and I'm going to liberate you from that foul spirit that's tormenting your mind. If you stay, and God doesn't deliver you, my wife and I will personally take you home."

She said, "You'll do that?"

I said, "I'll do it. I'll even go into your house first. You can stay with my wife in the car. I'll turn on every light, look behind the couch and the chairs, open your closet, and make sure there's nobody around there."

She was convinced. She said, "Well, if you'll do that, I'll stay."

After I preached that night, I called her up first for prayer. I laid hands on her and the power of God hit her and knocked her flat on her back. I laid hands on about 500 people that night.

After it was all over, my wife and I were looking for the woman because I'd promised to give her a ride home. But I couldn't find her anywhere! I ran outside and looked all over the place. I said, "Oh, Lord. I've got to find that woman." I never did.

The next night she came back into the meeting shouting and re-joicing. At night!

I said, "Come on up here. I know you've got a testimony."

She told the people the story I told you. She said, "I know Brother Schambach told me he and his wife would take me home last night. But I didn't have to let them take me home because when he laid hands on me, that devil of fear left. God delivered me and set me free! I walked the whole way home."

I said, "You walked? In Philadelphia?"

Now I was getting nervous! She lived 30 blocks away in South Philadelphia. That meant she had walked through the worst part of town! This was the same woman who was afraid to go out at night!

She said, "I got there at about 3 o'clock in the morning. I put the key in the latch, but I felt so good that I took it back out and walked the streets all night long saying, 'Devil, you're a liar. I'm not afraid of you anymore!'"

God delivered her from fear! If you are bound with a spirit of fear, He wants to do the same thing for you. You don't have to be afraid anymore. You can turn around and face the enemy with confidence because God is on your side!

Let me pray for you:

Father, in Jesus' name, I come to You on behalf of this one who's bound by fear. Thank You for the authority You've given me over devils. Fear, you foul, tormenting spirit, I adjure you by Jesus— loose your hold on this person's life. I command it in the name of Jesus. Lord, give him or her a miracle of deliverance, and give him or her the strength to stand up against the enemy. In Jesus' name, I call it done. Amen and amen.

CHAPTER 19

Singer Gets His Big Break

Glen Leonard grew up in the inner-city neighborhood of Washington, D.C. As soon as he discovered his natural gift for singing, he saw it as his ticket out of the ghetto. He believed his musical career was the answer for him.

At age 13, he began singing for local events. A little recognition eventually led to area, statewide, and national performances. One night, he saw five men singing on the *Ed Sullivan Show*. This group, The Temptations, made a big impression on him. He began to study them, dress like them, and sing like them.

By the time he was working with his third musical group, The Temptations had heard about Glenn and offered him a spot. He had finally made it.

It wasn't long before Glenn Leonard was singing lead. Yet, this man noticed a void in the core of his being. He was always seeking the adrenaline rush, but it would soon fade when the concert or recording session was over. The entertainer began looking for his next thrills in drugs, alcohol, and women.

One day, Glenn quit the group he had idolized for so long and began a solo career. He threw a three-day bash of drugs and alcohol to celebrate his brand-new solo release. On the last night of his binge, the oppression of emptiness reached an all-time low. He kicked all his party friends out of his hotel room and in his despair turned on the television to drown out the tormenting thoughts in his mind. Little did he know, he was at a turning point in his life.

"At the end of three days," Glenn remembers, "I was alone in a hotel room. A thought came to mind, 'What's gonna make this time different?' Fear came over me, and I turned on the TV. It was in the wee hours of the morning. As I flipped through the channels, I heard a man's voice. This man shouted at me from across the television."

As you might have guessed, that man was this same Holy Ghost preacher that Paul Deacock had heard on those records—Schambach! During that sermon, the Lord had moved on my heart and I said, "You, sitting in that hotel room. God has his hand on your life, son! Jesus is the One you are looking for!"

Then Glenn Leonard's miracle took place. It felt like somebody else was in that hotel room with him. It was the Holy Ghost! He had a supernatural encounter—the presence of Almighty God filled his room. Then, suddenly, after three days and nights of cocaine, marijuana, and champagne, he was finally sober.

Exhilarated by this unexplainable, supernatural experience, Glenn drove home to his wife and children. Immediately, he sought out a friend who had become a Christian. That friend led him to Jesus Christ, and within 15 minutes, Glenn was filled with the Holy Ghost. This happened on March 8, 1984.

His wife had been on the verge of leaving him. His new start not only set him free from despair, but God put His family back together, too.

The last time Glenn Leonard testified in one of my meetings, he and his wife and family were ministers of the Gospel. Instead of singing for The Temptations or for the devil, Brother Leonard is leading people to their new lives in Jesus Christ!

CHAPTER 20

Brother Leroy Gets Saved

In 1956 I was called back from the evangelistic field to bury my mama.

All of us remaining six kids were at her bedside when she died. She wasn't asking God to give her more life. My mother lived a full life. She had raised 12 kids. Six of us were left. Do you know what Mama was doing? She was crying out to God. She said, "Oh God, You promised me You would save all my children." Her dying cry was for her kids.

All of us were saved and filled with the Holy Ghost except my younger brother Leroy. He was six feet four inches and 240 pounds of solid steel. He was standing next to me at our dying mother's bedside. I gave him a poke in the ribs—almost broke my elbow.

I said, "Come on, boy. Get right with God before Mom goes."

He said, "Hey, not now. Mama is dying." He loved Mom just as much as anybody, but he was a backslider.

We buried Mom. She died without seeing that answer. Does that mean God isn't faithful? Of course not. I went back to the evangelistic field. I was traveling with Brother Allen all the time. We were in

California. I had a great burden for my brother. It hit me all of a sudden when Brother Allen was giving an altar call. I leaped off that platform. I jumped in the altar call for salvation.

Brother Allen said, "What are you doing there Schambach? The call is for sinners. It doesn't look good that my afternoon speaker is getting saved."

We are always making judgments on others, aren't we? We don't know what is going on in a person's heart. But I stayed there and said, "Lord, I am no longer R. W., I am Leroy. If he isn't going to get saved, I am going to get saved for him." Now, I had never heard anybody say that before, but I felt that. I wanted to get saved for him. I went into that prayer tent. I got on my face. I cried out to God.

The next day I had a call from my sister Margaret. I said, "Margaret, am I ever glad you called. I have some good news for you."

She said, "Will you let me talk? I am paying for this call."

I said, "You can talk when I get done. I have some good news. Leroy is saved!"

There was a silence on the phone.

I said, "Margaret, did you hear what I said?"

She said, "How did you know?"

I said, "How did I know? You don't know what I went through last night, girl." I told her how I took his place and answered the altar call, crying out to God to have mercy.

She said, "That's what I called to tell you. Last night we were all in church. All except Leroy. He was out living it up, having a ball. Halfway through the sermon, Leroy walked in. He didn't even stop to sit in a pew. He headed for the altar. He draped his six-feet-four frame over the altar and cried out to God. God saved him and filled him with the Holy Ghost."

Leroy didn't hear a sermon. Sometimes we preachers think we preach masterpieces. But people aren't getting saved because of the preaching. It is the Holy Ghost who takes them to the cross!

Chapter 21

Conclusion
"He'll Do It for You"

Do you need a miracle of deliverance today? I know God will do it for you if you'll let Him. I don't care what your situation is. I don't care how many times you've tried and blown it.

There are no "lost causes" in God's eyes; there are no irreversible situations. There is hope for every alcoholic, drug addict, liar, cheater, adulterer, murderer, or prostitute. It does not matter what the crime is. When a man or woman repents, a change takes place. That old, hardened criminal may deserve eternity in hell, but when he receives Jesus as Lord and Savior of his life, he becomes a child of God who will live in Heaven forever with Him. Hallelujah! What a miracle!

I was a young lad of 17 when my miracle came on a street corner in Harrisburg, Pennsylvania. I was running from God, busy going nowhere fast. As I rushed by on the way from work, I heard the voice of a street-corner preacher. It stopped me dead in my tracks. All of a sudden, over a loudspeaker, Brother Anthony Vigna cried out, "Hey, sinner!"

I thought, "Who knows me around here?"

So I leaned against a light pole and heard the preacher tell of Christ's love for me. He explained the plan of salvation for about 15 minutes. I learned that Jesus would forgive my past life of sin and give me complete cleansing in exchange. It was the greatest news I'd ever heard in my life.

Then came those life-changing words: "You don't have to sin anymore!" I was only 17, but I heard the words that brought freedom from guilt and from the bondage of sin.

There on that street corner, I fell to my knees, made an altar out of a curb, and surrendered my heart to Jesus Christ. People walking by laughed at me, but I didn't care. I asked Christ to forgive me, to cleanse me, to come into my life, and to walk and talk in me. I told Jesus I had turned my back on sin.

When I stood up, I had been cleansed and forgiven. I didn't know the theological term for what happened to me; it just felt like I had taken a shower on the inside. I was now a child of God. What a miracle! In an instant, I had passed from death to life.

God wants to do the same thing for you.

Jesus said, "…*Unless one is born again, he cannot see the kingdom of God*" (John 3:3). You must be born again!

I'm not talking about shaking a preacher's hand or putting your name on some church book. You might as well shake a donkey's tail and put your name on a barn door!

The only way to be saved is through Jesus Christ. Buddha is not the way. Mohammed is not the way. Hari Krishna is not the way. I'll take it one step further. The Virgin Mary is not the way! Jesus is the Only Way. He is the Way, the Truth, and the Life.

There is no purgatory. You're either saved or you're lost. You're either going to make heaven your home or you'll split hell wide open.

I know folks don't want to hear this kind of preaching. The church has changed its message: "Do the best you can. It'll all come out in the wash." You lying devil! It's not coming out in any wash. There's only one thing that can wash your sins away, and that is the blood of Jesus Christ!

This is the miracle of salvation. The blood of Jesus can wash away every sin! Romans 10:9 says, *"That if you confess with your mouth the Lord Jesus and believe in your heart that God has raised Him from the dead, you will be saved."*

If you want this miracle of salvation to take place in your life, then repeat this prayer after me:

> *Father, in Jesus' name, I come to You as a sinner. I confess my sin. I repent of my sin. I turn my back on sin. I've made up my mind that I'm going to serve the Lord and make heaven my home. Lord, I'm weak. I confess that to You. Make an entrance into my life by Your Spirit. Walk in me. Talk in me. Be my God, and let me be Your child. I believe in my heart, and I confess with my mouth that You raised Jesus from the dead. Lord, You said if I believe that and confess it, I'm saved. Thank You, Lord, for saving me. Amen.*

Now, if you prayed that prayer, then I believe you are a child of God. I want you to write me and let me know, because I have a booklet I want to send you absolutely free. It's called *You're One in a Million*. Request it when you write. It will tell you about the commitment you just made to God, and it will help you in your daily Christian walk with Him.

Glory to God! I hope these testimonies of deliverance have blessed your heart. But we're not done yet. Oh, no. We're just getting started!

PART III

Miracles of Healing

"The Lesser Is Included in the Greater"

As we have seen, the greatest miracle that can take place in an individual's life is when God reaches down His strong arm into the pit of sin, picks up a sinner, and washes him in the blood of Jesus Christ.

Now, I have learned in the science of logic that the lesser is included in the greater. That means if the greatest miracle is the salvation of the soul then all the other lesser miracles are included! If you can have faith for salvation, you can have faith for anything else that you may need. I believe this with all my heart.

Jesus Christ not only died on the cross to take away our sins, but He also took stripes on His back for our physical healing. Salvation and healing go hand in hand. You can't preach one without the other. If you preach salvation, you've got to preach divine healing.

In John 5:1-9, we read a great story of Jesus working a miracle of healing. Read it with me:

After this there was a feast of the Jews, and Jesus went up to Jerusalem. Now there is in Jerusalem by the Sheep Gate a pool, which is called in Hebrew, Bethesda, having five porches. In these lay a great multitude of sick people, blind, lame, paralyzed, waiting for the moving of the water. For an angel went down at a certain time into the pool and stirred up the water; then whoever stepped in first, after the stirring of the water, was made well of whatever disease he had. Now a certain man was there who had an infirmity thirty-eight years. When Jesus saw him lying there, and knew that he already had been in that condition a long time, He said to him, "Do you want to be made well?" The sick man answered Him, "Sir, I have no man to put me into the pool when the water is stirred up; but while I am coming, another steps down before me." Jesus said to him, "Rise, take up your bed and walk." And immediately the man was made well, took up his bed, and walked.

This is the story of a man who was sick and diseased for 38 long years, waiting for the troubling of the waters at the pool of Bethesda. In the Hebrew, Bethesda means "the house of mercy."

People brought the sick, the diseased, the blind, the maimed, and the dumb to this special place for just one purpose…for the troubling of the waters. When the angel stirred the water, the race was on! The person who moved fastest and reached the water the quickest would be made whole. And this poor man…

"I have no one to help me," he told Jesus. "There is always somebody pushing right by me to get into the water first!"

The heart of Jesus went out to this man. So Jesus commanded the man to "rise, take up your bed and walk." Immediately (I love that word "immediately"!), the man was made whole and walked. Even though he had been bound with this infirmity for 38 years, he was made whole instantly when Jesus spoke to him.

Jesus is a compassionate Savior. If the doctors have given up hope, and we cannot find one person to agree with us in prayer, Jesus is available. He gives hope to the hopeless. I have been an eyewitness to so many great miracles of healing throughout my ministry. A lot of folks may say He does not do it anymore. Let them talk all they want. I know He is still doing it be cause I have seen it with my own eyes.

Maybe you need a healing touch from God right now. I believe that as you read these next few stories, God is going to trouble the waters. The Holy Ghost is going to stir faith in your heart. Let that faith come alive inside of you, and get ready to receive your miracle from God.

I'm so thankful that we serve a God who heals! He is Jehovah Rapha! He is our Healer!

CHAPTER 22

Twenty-six Miracles

When I was on the Phil Donahue show, he asked me, "What is the greatest miracle you have ever seen?"

Of course, I told him the greatest miracle is that Jesus reaches down into the depths of sin, picks up a man and washes him in His blood, clothes him with His righteousness, and writes his name in the Lamb's Book of Life. That is the greatest miracle.

But what Phil wanted to know was what kind of healing or supernatural occurrence in the everyday world was the most dramatic move of God I have ever seen. And I have seen so many.

Oftentimes, I have seen miracles come as a result of a sacrificial offering. That doesn't mean we can buy a healing; but we can show faith with an offering, and God will take that faith and use it to meet our need. I'll never forget; the greatest miracle I ever witnessed began with an offering.

It happened under the ministry of Brother A. A. Allen. I was with this man of God for about five years in the '50s. When this great miracle happened, Dr. John Douglas and Brother Allen were together. I believe it was one of the greatest evangelistic teams of that day.

A woman brought her child, who had 26 major diseases, to our meeting. I'll never forget this as long as I live. The boy was born blind, deaf, and mute. Both arms were crippled and deformed. His elbows protruded up into his little tummy; his knees touched his elbows. Both legs were crippled and deformed; he had club feet. When he was born, his doctors said that boy would never live to see his first birthday, but they were wrong; he was approaching four years of age. Of course, his condition was breaking his mama's heart. She came to our meetings all week, and I got concerned about that boy. In those crusades, we had each person with a need fill out a prayer card, and as the Holy Spirit moved, we would pray for the needs God inspired us to pray for. And the Holy Spirit didn't seem to be moving us to pray for that little boy.

The following Sunday, his mother came to me and said, "Brother Schambach, I'm down to my last 20 dollars. I've paid the hotel bill, but we've been eating in the restaurant, coming to three services a day, and giving in every offering. All the money has run out. My baby has not been prayed for." She was very upset, and she was ready to go home.

I said, "Ma'am, I can't apologize for the moving of the Holy Ghost. I know you have to leave tonight, but if you come to the service and once again, the Holy Spirit leads in another direction, and your son's prayer card is not drawn for prayer, I will personally take your baby to the man of God's trailer house and see that he lays hands on your baby. You will not leave disappointed." And I meant that from my heart.

That night I came out, and I led the singing in that evening service. Then I introduced Brother A. A. Allen, and he came bouncing out on that platform and said, "Tonight we're going to receive an offering of faith." I had never heard him use that expression before, and I saw eyebrows lift all over the congregation. He went on, "Now, if you don't know what I mean when I say an 'offering of faith,' I mean for you to give God something you cannot afford to give. That's a good definition, isn't it? If you can afford it, there's no faith connected to it. So give Him something you can't afford to give."

As soon as Brother Allen said that, I saw that boy's mother leap out into the aisle and come running. Three thousand people were watching her in that Birmingham Fairgrounds Arena as she threw something in that bucket. I never saw anybody in such a hurry to give, and I confess, I was nosy. I came down off that platform to see what she had given. You know what I saw in that bucket? A 20-dollar bill.

I knew that was all she had. She had told me that. She had driven from Knoxville, Tennessee, to the meeting in Birmingham, Alabama. She didn't know how she was going to get home or what she was going to use to feed herself and her baby on the way. I went behind that platform and wept. I prayed, "Lord, I've been trying to teach that woman faith all week. But now I'm asking You to give me faith like she's got!"

I don't know whether I could have done what she did, and you don't know if you could do it. We will never know, unless we are in a similar situation. But Brother Allen went on and collected the offering and launched into his sermon. But about 15 minutes into his message he stopped and said, "I'm being carried away in the Spirit."

I said to myself, "Here we go again on another trip." This is how God used him: he said he could see what the Holy Spirit wanted to communicate to him like he was watching it on a television screen. He would describe it as he saw it. That night he said, "I'm being carried away to a huge white building. Oh, it's a hospital." Of course, I heard this kind of thing every night that I worked with Brother Allen, so I was sitting there unmoved.

Then he said, "I'm inside the hospital, and there's no doubt in my mind where I'm heading because I hear all these babies crying. It's a maternity ward. I see five doctors around a table. A little baby has been born. The baby was born with 12, no, 16, no, 26 diseases."

When he said that, I started getting chill bumps up and down my spine. I said, "Oh, my God, tonight's that baby's night!"

Brother Allen continued, "Twenty-six diseases. The doctors said he'd never live to see his first birthday, but that's not so. That boy is approaching four. Now I see the mother packing a suitcase. They're going on a trip. Another lady's with her. The baby's in a bassinet. It's in the back seat of an old Ford. They're driving down the highway. I see the Alabama-Tennessee border. That automobile is driving in the parking lot. Lady, you're here tonight. Bring me that baby! God's going to give you 26 miracles."

That woman came running again for the second time that night. She put the baby in Brother Allen's arms. I jumped up to stand beside him, and everybody in the audience—3,000 strong—was standing. Brother Allen must have wanted to be sure that the audience was agreeing in faith for the miracle because he said, "Everybody close your eyes." But I thought, *Not me, mister. I'm going to be scriptural on this one. I'm going to watch and pray. I've been waiting for this all week.*

That little boy's tongue had been hanging out of his mouth all week. The first thing I saw as Brother Allen prayed was that tongue snap back in the mouth like a rubber band. For the first time in four years, the little guy's tongue was in his mouth. I saw two little whirlpools in his eyes, just a milky color. You couldn't tell whether he had blue or brown or what color of eyes. But during the prayer, that whirlpool ceased, and I saw two brand-new brown eyes! I knew God had opened his eyes, and if God opened the eyes, I knew He had unstopped the deaf ears.

Then those little arms began to snap like pieces of wood; and for the first time, they stretched out. The legs cracked like wood popping. All of a sudden, I saw God form toes out of those club feet as easily as a child forms something with silly-putty. The crowd was watching by this time, going wild! I've never seen any people shout and rejoice so much in all my life.

I saw that baby placed on his feet, and he began to run for the first time in his life. He had never seen his mama before, never said a word, but he began running across the platform—and I was running right after him trying to catch him. He leaped into his mama's arms and I heard him say his first word: "Mama."

This miracle charged up the people of God so much that even more miracles began to happen there in Birmingham. We stayed for a week after that. People were bringing their handicapped friends and family members. There were about 12 or 13 people in wheelchairs over against one wall on the left side of the platform, and about 15 or so people who had been brought from the local hospital on stretchers on the right side of the platform. When everybody saw the power of God at work, all the handicapped people in wheelchairs stood up like a platoon of soldiers and walked out of there healed by the power of God, without hands ever being laid on them. Then 3,000 pairs of eyes, like they were being conducted by a conductor, looked in anticipation from the wheelchairs to the stretchers and got up and walked out of there healed by the power of God! Six blind people in the audience came running down the aisle with their white canes and threw them on the platform. Their eyes had been opened! Hearing aids began to pile up, then canes and crutches. Everybody in the building was healed.

It was an incredible time of miracles, and the power of God fell, starting with the 26 miracles for that one little boy. The following Saturday after his healing, I received a special delivery letter from his mother. She knew that I had a soft spot in my heart for her little son, so she wrote me. She said, "Brother Schambach, I took the baby to the hospital Monday morning, and the doctors won't give him back. They have kept him all week. They have called in every doctor from all over the country who has had anything to do with the case. They have pronounced my baby cured of 26 major diseases." Of course, we went on to get the copies of the affidavits from the doctors certifying that boy's life was a genuine miracle.

But there was a P.S. in that dear lady's letter, and a P.S. always means there's something more to the story. Her letter continued, "You remember that last Sunday when I told all I had was 20 dollars? God knows that was the truth. But when that man of God said to give something you can't afford, I leaped into the aisle. The moment I hit the aisle, for the first time in my life, I heard the devil talk. The devil told me, 'You can't give that; that's not yours. Fifteen dollars of that goes to the doctor. Five dollars is for gas to get home.' The faster I ran, the faster he talked. But as soon as I turned loose of that money, he stopped talking. Ain't no use talking now. It's gone! It's been put in the bucket now.

"Brother Schambach, all you saw was those 26 miracles, but there is one you don't know anything about. After you were gone, people were staying there. They wanted to see the baby and see what God had done. People shook hands with me. When one lady shook my hands, I felt a folded piece of paper between our palms. I opened it up and saw it was a 20-dollar bill. As I shook hands with the people who had lined up, every one of them had a folded paper in their hand. I went into the ladies room and counted $235!

"Isn't that just like God? He not only gave me 26 miracles for my baby, but He allowed me to stay in a hotel for a week, pay my bills, eat three meals a day in restaurants, give in three offerings every day, and still go home with more money than I came with!"

You can't beat God giving, no matter how much you try. Hallelujah! I believe with all my heart, as a result of what I saw, that the miracle had its origin in that gift of faith. When God dealt with that woman, she gave her last, and her last became her first.

CHAPTER 23

Hospital Riot in Newark

As previously mentioned, God works miracles in so many different ways. He uses many different vehicles to display His power in the lives of people. After all, He is a creative God.

One of these is anointing oil. The Bible teaches that oil is to be used to anoint for needs in the name of the Lord (see James 5:14). Now, the oil has no special power in itself, but God often works miracles through its use by the believer. I have seen this many times.

I have anointed many people and have seen God do miraculous things because of it. Then sometimes I distribute oil to other believers so that they can anoint others. I send out many bottles of oil absolutely free to those who request it for needs in their life.

In 1960 God led me to anoint people with oil during the crusade services. Sometimes I asked them to take their shoes off so I could anoint their feet. Then, I anointed their hands and their head. I would just pour oil on them.

In those days, I gave a bottle of oil to fired-up believers and sent them out with it. "Go out there and find somebody who is sick," I would tell them. "Anoint them with oil so that they may be healed." In reality, oil is a symbol of the Holy Ghost.

Years ago, during a crusade in Newark, I laid hands on a young man. On this particular night, I gave him a bottle of oil and spoke those same words to him. I didn't see him for a few nights. Then, his best buddy came and told me, "He is in jail."

"Why is he in jail?" I demanded.

He said, "For listening to you."

Now, if he was in jail because of what I had said, I wanted to go bail him out. But the Lord said, "Leave him alone." That is the trouble with us. We want to mess things up. Just let the Lord have His way.

On the fifth night, the missing man came bouncing into our meeting. I never saw a young man on fire like he was. I prayed, "Lord, if jail will do that for folks, put all these people in jail." He was on fire!

I called him to the front and gave him the microphone. I wanted to hear what he had to say. As it turned out, I didn't get to preach that night.

He told the audience that when I gave him the oil and told him to find someone who was sick, he didn't even go home. He went to the nearest hospital—where the sick were. He didn't have a minister's card. He wasn't ordained. All he had was a bottle of oil and an edict from the preacher saying, "Go find somebody who is sick."

He went to the hospital. It happened to be the largest hospital in the city. Without signing in with the nurse, he headed straight for the elevator. When he reached the 15th floor, he got the bottle of oil out and started laying hands on the sick. He told everybody he had laid hands on, "Get up and go home. God has healed you." He cleaned out the whole floor! Isn't that wild?

Those hospital patients had better sense than many church folks. They were going to do what the man of God told them to do, "Rise and walk."

After he got rid of the patients on that floor, he went down to the 14th floor. He was planning to anoint every patient in that hospital. Can you imagine folks going out the front door in slippers, pajamas, and overcoats and the nurses asking what they were doing? "The doctor said we were healed and told us to go home!"

The young man went to the next floor. He walked into a ward of about 180 people. There were five doctors working with a woman who had just passed away. The young man didn't run in. He waited until the doctors left. After the last doctor left, they pulled a sheet over the woman.

He went to her and pulled the sheet back. Everybody in the ward was looking in his direction. As they watched, the young man poured oil on the woman and rebuked death in the name of Jesus. He called her spirit back into her body. Suddenly, the woman sputtered about a half a dozen times and got up and out of the bed. She started shouting and running around the hospital room.

This, of course, isn't my story. I am just telling you what the young man told us. It blew us away. Can you imagine the chaos that broke loose in that ward? When you go in with a bottle of oil and something like this happens, they aren't going to ask you what church you represent or for your credentials. There was a dead woman jumping and screaming.

Every patient on that floor was saying, "Hey! Bring that oil over here. If it will raise that woman from the dead, it will heal me!"

This is the reason I anoint people with oil. I want to stir up that gift in them. When you do what God has called you to do, you will have people crying out for help. There is a world out there waiting for the Church to come alive. Today is the day we can say, "Look out, devil!"

But the young man's story isn't over yet.

The nurses called the police. They arrested the young man. He was charged with disturbing the peace. He was guilty—yes, he was. He was disturbing the devil's peace. Don't you think it is about time the Church disturbs the devil's peace? The devil has been disturbing our peace all along.

The authorities put him in jail and left him there for four days. The judge was aggravated when he saw the paperwork on the case. He said, "Why would this man be kept in so long?" He told them to go and get him out. When they brought him, the judge apologized to him. "Your Honor, don't apologize," the young man said. "Jesus put me there."

The judge was mystified. "I have heard everything blamed on Him, but never this," he replied.

The young man told the judge the story I just told you. He said, "Your Honor, when they arrested me I still had some oil left. I have gone to all the prisoners and anointed them—every one of them. Just five minutes ago the jailer got saved. You got me out just as I finished."

The judge looked over the bench. "Case dismissed," he said. Then he added, "Son, go get some more oil. God knows the Church isn't doing what He called it to do. Thank God there are young men being raised up to obey God."

I will never forget this story as long as I live. I tell it everywhere. Some folks don't believe it. But I just figure, they don't believe the Bible, why would they believe this?

Now you know why I anoint with oil.

CHAPTER 24

I Died on an Operating Table

I believe that God has a miracle for everyone who is sick. A lot of folks don't like this idea. They say, "Well, God put it on you to make you humble."

God doesn't put sickness on anybody! It's the devil that puts it on you. But God is going to take it off of you.

Still, there are skeptics. They might say, "Preacher, it's easy for you to tell people that God's going to heal them. But do you really know what they're going through?"

Well, I've got a story for the skeptics. I myself am a living testimony of the saving, healing, miracle-working power of God!

In 1987, my health was in serious jeopardy. I was facing quintuple bypass surgery for my heart. The doctors told me I wouldn't be able to preach anymore, and if I did I'd have to preach sitting down.

They shook their heads when they examined my X-rays; the blockage was extensive—87 percent blockage in one artery, 98 percent in another, 99 percent in yet another. My young doctor couldn't believe I was able to walk across the room, much less preach the way I do.

As someone who had preached faith and never taken aspirin, facing such a surgery was a frightening experience. I remember calling in my wife and grown children on the eve of the surgery. I couldn't predict the outcome, but we prayed and placed my health in the hands of the One who had been my Great Physician throughout my life.

Much later on, after the surgery, I found out that God had placed his ministering angels throughout the hospital. Spirit-filled nurses and attendants were stationed in the prep room, in surgery, in intensive care, and in recovery. When they saw I was in their unit, they prayed and interceded for me. All through that time of great testing, God was in control.

During surgery, I died on that operating table! It took the doctors almost five minutes to get my heart functioning again. My doctor, Dr. Cherry, didn't tell me this initially because he thought it might impede my recovery.

But when I later learned these things, I realized that God wasn't finished with me yet. He still had plans for me.

During my six-month recovery process, I had to learn new rest patterns and eating habits, and began exercising regularly. These are other ways in which I can treat the Lord's "temple" with respect. Even though I didn't drink alcohol or smoke, I had harmed my body through overeating, eating the wrong kinds of foods, and neglecting regular exercise.

Formerly, I thought all I had to do was pray over my food and keep on working for the Lord. Thank God for the new lessons I learned; and I also thank Him for His grace.

You see, after I started feeling better, I became a little careless. I started to let go of the rest patterns; I just worked harder. I didn't exercise as often—I let my flesh get the best of me. We must be faithful to care for the gift of life we've been given. God will do what we can't do.

About seven years after open-heart surgery, another illness hit—congestive heart failure. When Dr. Cherry called me into his office and I sat across from him, he was so pale he looked like he needed a doctor. He said, "Brother Schambach, you are going to have to stop preaching for a while. We need a miracle if you will ever preach again." He said I had lost a significant amount of my heart's functioning capacity and my body had filled up with fluid.

I don't mind telling you, that news hit me hard. The devil brought all kinds of thoughts to mind. He kept poking his ugly finger at me with thoughts of failure and death.

So, I would just talk back to the devil. "You've been a liar from the beginning, devil. I'm not finished yet. I'm just getting started! I'm in this for the long haul."

You see, if I really thought I wasn't going to preach anymore, I'd ask God to take me on home. This is what I was born for—to preach the gospel. But I knew that God was not done with me yet. I knew He still had plans for my ministry.

So even though Dr. Cherry pulled me off the road for three months, I got busy at home. I sent a letter to everyone I knew asking for prayer. Some preachers try to hide what they go through. But I hurt. I bleed. And I needed help. I wrote to my mailing list and said, "I've been praying for you for 40 years. Now I want some of it back. Pray for me." And they started praying.

I called every prayer line I could find. I wanted every bit of prayer I could muster up. Corporate prayer is a powerful tool against the devil. God cannot ignore the prayers of His people. As a result of the petitions to the Almighty, something supernatural happened.

I was scheduled for a visit to the doctor after three months of rest. I went back to Dr. Cherry and sat across from him. He looked a different color this time! He explained that with congestive heart failure, the best doctors can hope for is to maintain the level of failure without the heart losing any more of its functioning. Never with congestive heart failure do doctors see an increase in functioning.

Well, I've always served a God of the miraculous. Not only had my heart increased in functioning, but it had increased 65 percent! Dr. Cherry told my board members that he had seen many miracles, but mine was the greatest miracle he had ever seen.

He released me to go anywhere in the world! Anywhere! I don't have to slow down my pace. In fact, it's the younger people who work with me who have a hard time keeping up with my pace!

Praise God! The effectual, fervent prayers of God's people make a difference!

CHAPTER 25

You Don't Have Any Trouble

There is a powerful confession that I have learned to hold onto in the midst of difficult circumstances. It is something that I have said to countless people throughout the years. I close my broadcasts by saying it. It has become my motto…

You don't have any trouble…all you need is faith in God!

I learned that statement from a dear brother who had a personal encounter with the living Christ.

I was preaching in Buffalo, New York, when a gentleman invited me and my staff to his home for dinner. We enjoy invitations like that when we can because we get tired of quarter-pounders and French fries. One thing he forgot to tell me, however, is that he didn't live in Buffalo. He lived in Niagara Falls.

My meetings don't get out at nine o'clock. When you lay hands on thousands of people, it gets close to the midnight hour. After the meeting, we had to travel all the way to Niagara Falls. Whenever I am invited out, I fast all day. I make sure I don't eat anything because I like to fill up while I am there.

The man's wife had outdone herself with the menu. It was one of the most bountiful tables I have ever seen. She had roast turkey, porterhouse steak, roast beef, and fried chicken. (In that part of the country, you don't invite a preacher unless you have fried chicken.) The gentleman asked me to pray. I blessed the food.

We were anxious to start eating, but when the man began to speak, what he had to say was more interesting than the food. I actually pushed my plate back to listen. He said he had never been sick a day in his life. He had money in the bank. His future was secure. He worked for the government. But all of a sudden something struck him—spinal meningitis—and paralyzed him from head to toe. He spent over three months in the hospital. Doctors were called in from all over the world. His bank account dwindled. He had to sell his home for the equity to pay the doctor bills. Rheumatoid arthritis crept into every joint until he couldn't stand the pain. He lapsed into a coma for almost four months.

Since the man was Roman Catholic, his priest was called to administer the last rites of that church. Lying in the coma, he knew what the priest was doing, but he couldn't communicate because he was paralyzed. "I couldn't flicker an eyelash," he recalled. How would you feel when you know that the priest is giving you the last rites— the last ceremony in the Catholic church before you die?"

As soon as the priest left, another priest walked through the wall and over to the bed. There was something different about this priest. He was dressed all in white. The new priest leaned down to the dying man and called him by name. He said, "You don't have any trouble. All you need is faith in God."

Of course, he was laying there thinking, "What kind of crazy priest is this? I don't have any trouble? Here I am in a coma. I can't communicate. There is arthritis in every joint. I have spinal meningitis. I had to sell my home. My bank account is gone. Is this not trouble?"

But the priest said, "I am Jesus of Nazareth, and I am going to heal you right now."

Isn't that beautiful? Jesus said, "When I walk out of this room, I want you to get out of this bed. Shave, wash, and walk out of this hospital. Go to the first bookstore you can find and buy a Bible. Start reading from St. John's Gospel. You will find the way to eternal life."

Oh, hallelujah! The man told us that Jesus turned and walked right back through the wall. As the man was telling me this story, he looked at me and said, "Brother Schambach, I wonder why Jesus didn't just use the door."

I said, "He is the door!"

He can make an entrance wherever you are. He can come right into your automobile. He can visit you on your job. He can walk into your bedroom. No matter where you are, Jesus is the door. He will come in!

When Jesus walked out of that room, the man got out of bed and started shaving. The nurse came tip-toeing in. She wanted to pull the sheet over because the other priest had walked out. But she saw the bed empty. She ran into the bathroom and said, "Please get back into bed. Don't you know you are dying? The priest gave you the last rites."

The man said to her, "Cool it, honey. Another priest came in and gave me the 'first rites' all over again. I am going to live!"

When you have an experience with God, you are never at the mercy of a man with an argument. People will come to you and say, "I don't believe in healing." All you have to do is laugh and say, "Then you can stay sick. But my God healed me."

CHAPTER 26

Sharon's New Eye Miracle

My wife and I pastored a church in the early 1950s. A man, who later became a dear friend of mine, used to bring his six-year-old daughter to Sunday school. He would always drop her off, and I would wonder who her parents were. But he would never come to Sunday school. He would never come to church.

One day I jumped in front of his car to stop him. I wanted to talk to him. But he knew who I was, and that was the last time I jumped in front of his car. He put it in gear and laid the rubber down. I flew into the bushes. He didn't want to talk to the preacher.

I was after that big fish. I liked that little girl coming to Sunday school, but I wanted the father to come also. However, he couldn't bring himself to come to church. I knew he was a sinner. Sinners don't like to go to church.

One day my wife and I were on vacation visiting her mother in Philadelphia. I got a long-distance phone call. I heard a strange voice on the other end of the line. The man had tears in his voice. He said, "Brother Schambach?"

I said, "Who is this?" It was that little girl's father. I said, "Oh, something must be wrong. You called me brother. You tried to run over me last time we met. What is wrong?"

He said, "I am in the hospital in McKeesport, Pennsylvania."

I said, "What is wrong with you?"

"Nothing is wrong with me. It is my daughter."

That daughter was the apple of her daddy's eye. "What happened?" I asked.

He told me that his family was visiting them. While the children were playing in the backyard, her cousin picked up a rusty nail and threw it. It was an accident, but it hit his daughter in the eye and shattered the eyeball. The doctors wanted to cut the eye out.

"Well," I said, "let them operate."

He said, "She told me to call you!"

I said, "What would you like me to do?" I wanted him to lay it on the line.

"She wants you to come and bring that bottle of oil. She says that if you pray for her, everything will be all right."

Kids have faith! "Well," I said, "I am thankful she wants me to come. I am her pastor. What about you?"

He said, "Please come."

I replied, "I am on the way. Don't let the doctors operate. Don't let them do anything until I get there." I took the next plane out.

I had visited that hospital practically every day in the past. Doctors there knew me on a first name basis. I would pray and minister to the sick. Two of the young interns met me at the entrance. They said, "Hurry up and do your thing. An infection is setting in the eye. We have to take her to the operating room and remove the eye."

I said, "Now, hold on, fellows. What makes you think that after I do my thing you are going to have to do your thing? That is why I have been called. That girl is expecting a miracle!"

Children believe God. I would rather lay hands on a child than on an adult any day. It is the adults I have problems with. Children believe anything you tell them. The adults, however, deal with logic all the time. They want to know what makes it work. They want to logically figure it out. That is why adults often get nothing from God. A child just says, "Pray for me, and I will be all right."

The interns said, "We aren't going to argue with you. Go in anyway."

I didn't go in the room. I headed for the waiting room because I knew her father would be there. I wasn't about to go in and pray for that girl. I wanted that man first. He wasn't going to run over me anymore.

There he was. He was weeping. His daughter was suffering.

I said, "I finally caught up with you. Get on your knees. It is time to pray now."

The two doctors came in and said, "Will you please come with us? The trouble isn't here, it is inside."

I answered, "That is why you are a doctor and not a preacher. You don't even know where the trouble is. I have been after this guy for about nine months. I am not about to let this fish go now. Get on your knees, brother. We are getting right with God."

I didn't have to beg him. He fell on his face. He prayed, and we touched God. God saved him and gave him a miracle in his life. After God transformed him, I said, "Let's go now." We headed for Sharon's room. I will never forget her. She was a pretty little blond girl. There she was, lying on her bed with a patch over her eye. When I stepped in, she turned to me and smiled. "I knew you would come," she said softly. "Everything is all right now."

I got out my bottle of oil and walked toward her. There were two doctors standing next to me. They said, "What are you doing?" I got my bottle out and put oil on her. They were looking at the oil saying, "Can I look at that? What is this, holy oil?"

I said, "No. I got it from my wife's kitchen. She fries chicken in it. I bought it at the A & P. There isn't anything holy about the oil. Oil can't heal you. You can go swim in oil and it won't heal you."

And the prayer of faith will save the sick, and the Lord will raise him up. And if he has committed sins, he will be forgiven (James 5:15).

There is something about a child who just believes God. I didn't want to answer all those questions, so I said to the doctors, "Please wait outside, will you? Wait until I get done. You don't let me in your operating room, so please step out of mine."

They went out. I didn't even bother to look at the eye. I didn't have to look at it—I wasn't the doctor. I laid hands on her and said a simple prayer. I didn't even shake. I said, "Father, in the name of Jesus, perform the miracle and give her a new eye." That is all I said. I turned to the door and saw the two doctors. I waved for them to come in.

They asked, "Can we have her now, Reverend?" They were getting testy with me now. They had never called me Reverend before.

I said, "What are you going to do with her?"

"Well, we told you the eye is infected. We have to cut it out."

I said, "It isn't infected anymore."

"What are you talking about?"

I said, "Didn't you tell me that the eye was shattered in a hundred pieces? You said that. I never even looked at it."

"Why, of course, that is why we have to operate."

I said, "You don't have to take her anymore. God just performed a miracle." I knew that little girl had faith. I knew God wasn't going to disappoint that faith. He never disappoints faith.

They said, "What do you mean?"

I said, "Look at the eye."

They went over, took the bandage off, and took a peek at it.

"I don't believe it!" the doctors exclaimed.

I said, "That is the reason I had you stand outside the door. You can't believe it even when you look at it."

Jesus said, *"Blessed is she who believed, for there will be a fulfillment of those things which were told her from the Lord"* (Luke 1:45).

God is looking for men and women who will stand on His Word believing that if He said it, He will do it, and that if He spoke it, He will bring it to pass. God has to take you outside that human realm in order to do something supernatural.

CHAPTER 27

Dying Baby Healed

There was a coal miner who had a precious little baby boy. He and his wife had agreed that he was going to be in the delivery room when this child was born. They had two other children, but he wanted to witness the birth of this one.

It is a good thing he was in the delivery room, because there were complications. The doctor panicked and told the husband, "Press down on your wife's stomach and force that baby out."

Of course, the husband didn't know about delivering babies, and he was also panicking. But he did what the doctor said. He pushed down on the stomach, and the baby shot out through the hands of the doctor and landed on the floor. The doctor picked up the baby nervously and accidentally hit the baby's head on the edge of the table. There was a hole in the baby's head, and terrible brain damage had occurred.

The man later told me, "I was in that delivery room—saved, sanctified, and filled with the Holy Ghost—but when I saw what the doctor did to my baby, I wanted to kill her."

It took a lot for him to confess that. It shows that you never know what is in a person's heart. It doesn't matter how well you speak in tongues. There is only one step from the spiritual to the carnal. This man had murder in his heart. He wanted to kill the doctor for hurting his baby.

But the young father's story doesn't end with a heart full of murder. Jesus appeared to him in that room and said, "Son, I can't do anything for you if you act like this."

When the young man told me this, he said, "Praise God, He still called me 'son,' even when I had murder in my heart!"

In other words, when you are in the carnal, God can't do anything for you. So, do you know what this man did? He walked right up to the doctor and said, "Please forgive me for talking to you like that. I am so sorry. Jesus just told me He is going to heal my baby."

The doctor, full of despair, replied, "Oh, your baby is going to die."

But the man said, "Oh no, my baby isn't going to die. Jesus said He is going to heal him."

She said, "If your baby lives, he will be a human vegetable. He won't be able to talk."

But the couple took that baby home. The father went to the bank and borrowed money for plane tickets to fly from Pittsburgh to Atlanta where we were holding meetings. They brought their baby to the crusade. The poor little guy had a plastic tube draining fluid off his brain. They unhooked his pajamas and showed me the spine outside his body, with some kind of plastic flesh sprayed over it by the doctors. I had never seen anything like it. The baby had spina bifida. His little toes were turned upward into his legs, making his feet look like clubs.

I put that baby in my hands before I preached and walked across that platform for about 20 minutes. I felt the anointing of God like I have never felt it before. In my spirit I knew God had healed that baby. Still, there was no evident sign. It takes faith to believe God when you can't see the signs.

I say this to encourage you. If you don't see immediate results, don't panic. Hold on to God's Word.

There was no immediate result. I put the baby back in his father's hands and said, "God has healed your baby! Take him home." The man didn't shout. In fact, he looked confused because the baby didn't look any different.

They took the baby back to the hospital. The doctor was there when the father checked the baby in. "You shouldn't have taken this baby out of the hospital," the doctor said. "He is worse!"

"That is what I thought," the man said, "but the preacher told me the baby is healed!"

The doctor said, "He must be a crazy preacher!"

But you see, the Bible says this is foolishness to the natural man. The natural man can't receive anything from God. It is foolishness to him.

So the downhearted father left the baby in the hospital and went back to work in the coal mines. As he picked up his pick and shovel, Jesus came into the coal mine. He looked directly at him, and said, "Son, why are you doubting Me? I have healed your baby."

The pick went one way and the shovel went another. He ran out of the mine, got on the telephone and called his wife. "Honey, get dressed! We are going to the hospital to get our baby. Jesus just stopped by the coal mine and told me He healed him!"

"I know it!" his wife replied. "Before He came to the mine, He came to me and told me the same thing!"

They went to the hospital and the father to the doctor, "Get my baby ready! He is healed! I am taking him home!"

The doctor said, "Have you been talking to that crazy preacher again?"

"No!" the father answered. "I have been talking to the Man this time. When you get it from headquarters, you are healed!"

The baby wasn't healed right away. The court ordered those parents to take the baby to the Pittsburgh Children's Hospital. But this too was God's plan because this case is on record there. Sixteen doctors looked at that baby. While the greatest specialists on spina bifida checked that baby, God pushed the spine back into the baby's body and reduced the fluid in his head.

Later, I was preaching in Rex Humbard's church in Akron, Ohio. Sitting on the front row were the baby's parents with their baby boy. The proud father was waving happily at me, saying, "Hallelujah!"

The doctors had said the baby would be a vegetable, but he was healed by the power of the living Christ!

CHAPTER 28

Oxygen Tank Miracle

A young 17-year-old girl in New York was dying with tuberculosis. One lung had collapsed. The other one was half gone. She was in an oxygen tank.

She attended a denominational church. The folks in her church loved God and were saved. However, they didn't believe in divine healing. Of course, divine healing doesn't make us Christians. The blood of Jesus makes us Christians because He paid the price for our salvation at Calvary.

This young girl was dying. Her physician, who was a Christian, told her, "You are going to die, and there is nothing we can do. Tuberculosis has set in. One lung is gone. The other is half gone. I am going to send you home so that you can spend your remaining days with your family."

She was breathing pure oxygen. She lay in an oxygen tent waiting for death. She was 17 years old and had dwindled to 67 pounds. She was a lovely young lady, but she was wasting away. Don't you tell me God does that to folks. I wouldn't serve a God who did that. God is a good God. He promises beauty for ashes.

The thief does not come except to steal, and to kill, and to destroy. I have come that they may have life, and that they may have it more abundantly (John 10:10).

The doctor sent the girl home to die. She lay there with her head up so she could read her Bible. She resigned herself to the fact that she was going to die. This is what she had been taught. You are only what you are taught. That is why you have to be careful where you go to church. I can't say that strongly enough. The girl lay in that position, reading Peter's epistle, *"Who Himself bore our sins in His own body on the tree, that we, having died to sins, might live for righteousness…"* (1 Pet. 2:24). When she read those words, she put her Bible down and began to praise God.

Weeping, she said, "Oh, Lord, I will be so glad to see You. I know I am going to die. Doctors can't do any more for me. But thank You for saving me. Thank You for washing me in the blood." She worshiped and thanked God for saving her and went back to reading the same verse she had just read in the Bible.

"Himself bore our sins in His own body on the tree, that we, having died to sins, might live for righteousness…" But she didn't stop there this time. She went right on in that same verse, *"…by whose stripes you were healed."* The words lit up like a neon sign. She said, "Oh, look what I found." There was no preacher there to preach to her. No one was there but the Word. She said, "Lord, I just finished praising You for the first part, now I am going to praise You for the second part. You have already healed me. Jesus, I am sorry I won't be seeing You right now. I plan on staying around here awhile."

Isn't that beautiful faith? Hallelujah! "I won't be coming like I planned," she said. "I have changed my mind because I just found some truth—and truth is what sets us free." She started praising God for perfect health. She didn't gain weight instantly. She still weighed 67 pounds. She unzipped that oxygen tent and hollered for her mother. "Mama, come quick!"

Her mother thought this was the day her daughter was going to die. She came stumbling up the stairs. "What is it, baby? What is it?"

"Oh, Mama, look what I found. Read this."

Her mother mumbled through the words, then said, "I read it. Lay down now."

The daughter said, "Oh, you didn't read it right. Won't you read it? Mama, it says I am healed. Two thousand years ago Jesus healed me."

Isn't it strange how some people can read it and get nothing out of it? The mother looked at her daughter and started crying.

"What is wrong, Mama? What are you crying about?"

"The doctor told me that on the day you were to die, you would lose your mind."

Isn't it strange that when you want to trust God, people think you are losing your mind? When you are willing to die, you are normal. "It is all right to get religious, but you don't have to carry that too far. Don't be a fanatic!" You don't have to believe that.

Her mother tucked her back in. But the girl said, "Mama, I am not going to die. Go downstairs and make me breakfast. I want some bacon and eggs, orange juice, whole wheat toast, and coffee."

Mama said, "Now I know you have lost your mind. You haven't eaten anything in ten months."

She said, "I haven't heard such powerful truth in ten months. Go down and make my breakfast. I am getting out of here."

The girl's mother tucked her in and sneaked out of the room. No sooner had she closed that door than the girl unzipped the oxygen tent. She pulled her scrawny legs out of the bed and hobbled over to her dresser. She took one of the dresses that she had worn when she was 120 pounds. It looked like a robe on her now. She put slippers on her feet and started down the stairs. She went to the kitchen, opened that door and asked, "Are my bacon and eggs ready?" She sat down to have breakfast and said, "Lord, bless this food to my brand-new body. I am not going to die. I am going to live."

She went to her doctor the next day. The X-rays found two brand-new lungs and no sign of tuberculosis.

She went on to live in New York. She married and gave birth to four children. This was all possible because she heard the truth.

People say, "My church doesn't believe it"—but neither did hers. Her mother wouldn't even believe with her. You don't need anybody—all you need is the Word of God. Stand on that Word.

CHAPTER 29

Man Wrapped in Sheet

I was preaching in Houston, Texas, when a woman walked into my meeting with a sheet on her shoulder. I wondered what she had in that sheet. It wasn't long before I found out, because she walked down the center aisle and dropped it at my feet. I was preaching—she was messing up my service! When she opened the sheet, there was a man in it—her husband. He weighed only 58 pounds.

She said, "My husband used to weigh 200 pounds." Now he looked like a human skeleton. The stench of the man's disease almost knocked me out. I knew it was cancer. The woman looked at me and said, "It took me all night to get here, preacher. Now do what God called you to do. Heal this man."

These are the types of situations that help you find out whether you are called and sent, or whether you just went.

The woman said, "I come from New Orleans. The doctor told me yesterday my husband has 72 hours to live. One of those days is already shot. That means we only have 48 hours. When the doctor told me the news, I told him I was taking my husband to Houston. He told me there was no use in taking him to Houston. He thought I wanted to bring him here to the cancer specialists, and he said they would give me the same bottom line—that my husband is going to die. I just told the doctor, 'That is what you think.'"

That is the truth about faith, isn't it? Sometimes you have to stand alone.

The doctor told her he wouldn't let her move the patient, but she said, "He is my husband. I will sign him out." That is the kind of woman to have. Most women would try to get rid of the old rascal. But she said, "He is my man. I am not going to let that devil have him."

The doctor said, "Those specialists are going to give you the same diagnosis I did."

She said, "I am not taking him to a specialist. I am taking him to a man of God."

He said, "A what?"

"A man of God."

He said, "I don't believe in that."

She said, "You don't have to. He is my man. I believe in it. That is the bottom line."

Let every man, let every devil be a liar, but let God be true! If He said it, He will do it, and if He spoke it, He will bring it to pass!

She said, "I am going to sign him out."

The doctor said, "I will hide his clothes."

She said, "I will steal a sheet."

I looked at the sheet, and it had the name of the hospital on it. She had stolen it! Faith never gives up. Faith will find a way. Faith presses on. Faith takes the answer from God. Faith never sits in a pew. Faith steps out on the water. Faith steps out on the Word. Faith says, "Yes, Lord, I am going to take the answer." God can't lie. I believe what He said.

She said, "Brother Schambach, let's dispense with the talking now. Lay your hands on him."

I couldn't stand to look at him because the stench was coming right at my face. I had to turn my face, but I touched him. I said, "You foul devil. I curse you at the roots in the name of Jesus, and I command you to die and pass from this man's body."

That man was only in his late forties. The devil kills people before their time. The thief comes to steal, to kill, to destroy. I could see the marks of the devil on that body, but I refused to let the devil have him. I said, "In the name of Jesus, I reverse it." I threw the sheet on him and said, "Get him out of here. He is well."

He didn't get up and walk. He only weighed 58 pounds—skin and bones. The woman picked him up, threw him right back over her shoulder, walked out, didn't even stay for the offering. Halfway back, she turned around and said, "Bye, Brother Schambach. See you when you get to New Orleans."

Six months later we put the tent up in New Orleans. During the opening night, I saw a big man enter. He was six-feet-one and weighed 200 pounds. He wore a brand-new blue suit. I didn't know who he was. He walked up on the ramp, and I wondered why my men let him get up there. The Holy Ghost must have frozen them right in their spot. We don't let anybody up on the platform. All of a sudden, this guy grabbed me and lifted me off the ground. I said, "Put me down."

He said, "I am the man who was in the sheet."

I said, "Pick me back up again. Let's dance!"

Isn't that beautiful? Six months later, he was back to his normal weight. He hadn't even known his wife had taken him to Houston. He was just about gone, 48 hours to live. When she took him back to the doctor, they examined him and couldn't find a trace of cancer anywhere. When I spoke to that cancer, I spoke resurrection life into his body. I spoke to that mountain. I spoke in faith believing God was going to do it. I called it done. If God says He is the

Healer, I have a right to pronounce him healed. Speak it into existence in the name of Jesus.

> *For we do not wrestle against flesh and blood, but against principalities, against powers, against the rulers of the darkness of this age, against spiritual hosts of wickedness in the heavenly places* (Ephesians 6:12).

> *Five of you shall chase a hundred, and a hundred of you shall put ten thousand to flight; your enemies shall fall by the sword before you* (Leviticus 26:8).

Why?

> *You are of God, little children, and have overcome them, because He who is in you is greater than he who is in the world* (1 John 4:4).

CHAPTER 30

Spit in My Eyes

A black lady, who had been blind for 38 years, was in New York city. She was standing in line ready to receive prayer. There were about 500 people to pray for—and the ushers brought her first. After I prayed, I said, "I believe God. It is done. You are healed."

She said, "No, I am not."

I put my arm to her back and I tried to move her along but she just dug in. She said, "I am not going anywhere. You didn't do what God told me to tell you to do."

I said, "Take it by faith."

She said, "No." She just stayed there. She said, "Brother Schambach, God told me to tell you to do something. I am not leaving here until you do it."

I said, "All right, what did He tell you?"

She said, "He told me to tell you to spit in my eyes."

I said, "I am not going to do that. It isn't sanitary. It isn't healthy. I am not going to do it."

She said, "Yes, you are, because I am not leaving until you do. God told me to tell you to do this."

She wouldn't budge. I said, "I won't do it. I am not spitting on you."

She said, "Brother Schambach, I am tired of being blind. Jesus did this to heal a blind man. Are you better than Jesus?"

She knew how to hurt a guy. I said, "I am going to find out if God really spoke to you."

She wouldn't give up. Thank God for women who don't give up. Don't you take no for an answer. If you find something in the Book, stick by your guns. Say, "Devil, you are a liar." Show your faith to God. Say, "God, look what You said here. You can't lie. If You said it, then it belongs to me. I am going to write my name right there on the side of the margin, 'Lord, it belongs to me.'"

The woman refused to give up. She knew God's voice. I began to weep. But I did what God had told her should be done. And the moment I did, the power of God hit her. For the first time in 38 years, 20-20 vision came back to her eyes. She ran around that building!

Don't give up. Don't give up. Whatever He says for you to do, do it. God is looking for obedience.

CHAPTER 31

Doubly Good

I love it when a doctor examines somebody that he said had cancer, and after prayer they can't find it. I love to see the doctor scratching his head when the power of God throws a wrench in all his medical knowledge.

And my speech and my preaching were not with persuasive words of human wisdom, but in demonstration of the Spirit and of power, that your faith should not be in the wisdom of men but in the power of God (1 Corinthians 2:4-5).

This is what I preach. I don't fill people's heads with elegant words. Too many preachers spend all their time telling God's people about things. I like to *show* them. I like to demonstrate the Gospel of power. I love to see those doctors scratching their heads.

Now, there are many doctors who are men of faith. God uses them in their field, I know. But I believe God likes to amaze even the doctors. He likes to let them know that He's still God—that He's the Great Physician.

In Hobbema, Alberta, Canada, I preached the Word of God on an Indian Reservation. I was encouraging the people to give to God.

I'll never forget this one Indian brother who was there. He had his daughter with him, who was diagnosed with cancer of the cervix. That night he gave to God. He made a faith promise, believing that God would meet his financial need and heal his daughter.

The next day, he called me at the motel I was staying in. It was the only one in town.

He said, "Brother Schambach."

I said, "Who is this?"

"I was in your service yesterday," he replied. "I just had to call you."

I wondered how he knew where I was. I asked him, "How did you find me?"

He said, "There's only one motel in this town. I knew you had to be here since you're not at the tent. They put me through to you. I just had to tell you something. I made that faith promise and gave to God. I was obedient to what you said. Well, I went to work this morning and my employer put a $20,000 check in my hand!"

He woke me up! I said, "Hold the phone while I shout with you a little bit!"

While I was shouting he said, "Now, don't get too carried away. I'm not done yet. My daughter, who had cancer of the cervix, went back to the doctor. And he's scratching his head. He said, 'I don't know where the cancer's gone, but the cancer has disintegrated in a matter of 24 hours.'"

That's greater than $20,000. That's greater than all the money in the world!

These are the kinds of miracles that God is doing. It's the manifestation of His Spirit in this Last Day. I call it "exhibition." I like that word. Preachers of the Gospel must place the power of the Living God on exhibition. It's time we exercise our faith and demonstrate this power that we have been given!

CHAPTER 32

Forty Tumors and a Handkerchief

Sometimes we must exercise our faith for "special miracles."

As mentioned in Acts 19:11-12:

> *Now God worked unusual miracles by the hands of Paul, so that even handkerchiefs or aprons were brought from his body to the sick, and the diseases left them and the evil spirits went out of them.*

Paul traveled continually from place to place as he ministered. People were healed and delivered from the power of evil spirits. As a result, the news this power spread all over the country.

There were multitudes of people who needed healing and deliverance who couldn't get to him so the Spirit of the Lord instructed him to take cloths from his body and send them to those in need.

The anointing of God's power on those cloths was so strong that the people who received them were healed and delivered. The cloth became a faith trigger, a power release for special miracles.

Like Paul, I wear cloths on my body. God promised me that as I wore these pieces of cloth on my body, the same anointing that was on me as I ministered would penetrate these cloths, and they would become anointed cloths.

There is no magic in the cloth. We all wear cloth, so if there was magic in it, we'd all be healed already. That prayer cloth serves as a point of contact, allowing me to unite my faith with those who are in need.

I know some of you think prayer cloths are a bit strange. But God's Word specifically ordains their use. And that's good enough for me. If the Bible told me to stand on my head to receive my miracle, I'd do it!

I was preaching in Philadelphia one year. After the service, a woman named Arlene came to me with a strange question. She asked me if she could have my handkerchief. So I gave it to her.

What I didn't know was that Arlene had learned from the doctors that she had 40 cancerous tumors in her breast.

But her faith in God was strong. When she was watching me preach, she saw me take my handkerchief out and wipe the sweat from my brow. That made her think of the scripture in Acts that we just read. She asked me for my handkerchief, and I gave it to her.

One year later I was holding a tent crusade in Philadelphia. Wouldn't you know, this same woman came to the platform with a testimony. She told the people about the special miracle that God performed.

"With over 40 cancerous tumors in my breast, I was facing either radiation treatments or a total mastectomy. Then, Brother Schambach came to town and I went to his meeting. As he preached, I watched him take his handkerchief out and wipe his brow, and I thought of the scripture about Paul's handkerchiefs being laid on the sick and they recovered.

"After the meeting, I asked Brother Schambach if I could have his handkerchief. The moment he handed it to me, I felt God's anointing go all through my body…and I was healed! That happened last year, and since then I have had several body scans, with no trace of cancer."

Arlene still carries that handkerchief with her everywhere she goes and just keeps on praising the Lord for what He did for her.

CHAPTER 33

Chain Reaction

I have a dear friend, Brother Alvaro Fernandez, a Latin-American brother who lives in Norway. He and his wife have been such a blessing to my ministry. When we held revival meetings in Russia, it was Brother Fernandez who coordinated the whole thing.

It blesses me to see young ministers like him walking in faith and doing the works of Christ across the globe. But that faith of his was put to the test a number of years ago. The devil wanted to rob him, but God performed a miracle.

Eight months after he and his wife, Elizabeth, were married, the doctors discovered that she had a tumor on her lungs. She went into extensive chemotherapy to treat the cancer. The doctors didn't give her much hope. This was a very difficult time for both of them.

It was during this time that I asked Brother Fernandez to help me with my Russian Crusade. He agreed and began the work. His wife, although very sick, didn't stay in bed. She went with him. She had to wear a turban on her head because of the chemotherapy.

In May of that year, I met them in Russia. I prayed for that dear woman, and you know what? God healed her! Three months later, the doctors took another test. The tumor was totally gone, and all that remained was a mark inside where it had been. The doctors said it was as if someone had removed the cancer from her body. Hallelujah! I know who that Someone was. It was Jesus Christ!

But that wasn't all God had in store.

The chemotherapy had damaged Elizabeth's womb so badly that she could not have any children. The doctors said it would be impossible. Well, they were wrong.

One year later, Brother and Sister Fernandez visited the United States. When I saw them, I laid hands on her again. "I bless the fruit of her womb."

Now, they were perplexed by this, since the doctors had told her she could not have any children. But I serve a God who likes to confound the doctors!

When they went back to Norway, Elizabeth was feeling a little strange. So the doctors took a picture of her womb. To their amazement, something was there!

They couldn't believe this, so they started checking her for cancer again. But glory to God, it wasn't cancer! It was a baby!

Now they have two precious children, Samuel and Victoria Joy. God has blessed that family for their faithfulness to Him.

But the story is not over yet!

Some time later, it was discovered that Elizabeth had a form of heart disease. You know, the devil just can't take a hint! You think he'd learn by now that he can't put his filthy hands on God's people and get away with it. God had another miracle waiting in the wings.

When they discovered that she had heart disease, they sent notice to me. I was conducting meetings in Long Island at the time. So I sent a prayer cloth to them.

When the prayer cloth touched her, she was totally healed and restored. And God did more than just that! While she was in the hospital, she was reading the stories in my book *Miracles* (many of which are also in this book). She gave it to the lady in the bed beside her to read. When that lady read those stories of God's miracle-working power, she got saved and was healed of her infirmity!

See, the devil doesn't have any sense. What the devil intended for evil, God worked out for good. God set off a chain reaction for Brother and Sister Fernandez. He just kept on working miracles! You see, it doesn't matter what the report of the doctors is. What matters is the report of the Lord. If He says you are healed, then you *are* healed!

CHAPTER 34

What the Best Doctors Couldn't Do

If the devil can't get to you, sometimes he goes after your family. A family emergency can knock the wind out of even the greatest man of faith, and the devil knows that. He doesn't care how he gets you. He'll just try to pull you down whatever way he can.

In 1993, the devil went after the family of a dear brother, Reverend Joe Martin, who pastored a church in Virginia Beach, Virginia, where I was conducting a ten-day tent crusade.

Brother Martin sponsored these meetings. He had been preparing for four hectic weeks. So by the time the crusade rolled around, he and his wife, Kathy, and their eight children were exhausted (his wife was pregnant with their ninth child also).

On October 7, the night before the crusade began, their 18-month-old daughter, Elisha Ann, started having difficulty breathing. She started coughing with something. It was just a bad cold, so they passed it off for a while.

By Sunday night, the problem had grown more severe, and they noticed a rattle in her lungs. She could hardly breathe and couldn't drink milk. So they took her to the doctor the next morning.

There were four specialists at the hospital at the time. They listened to her lungs and looked at her heart on a special heart sonogram. The doctors just looked at each other in silence and then told the father how serious it was.

"This is not bronchitis. This is not a whooping cough. Your daughter has a congenital heart defect, a cardiac myopathy, and all four chambers of the heart have failed. This is blood in her lungs. One-third of the patients with such a heart defect have heart transplants or die, one-third stay the same with medicine, and one-third get better."

They told him that his daughter would live on increasing doses of medicine until she died unless she had a heart transplant.

"You're wrong," Brother Martin told them.

Then all four specialists looked him in the eye. "I wish we could say we're wrong, but we all agree."

So they took their little daughter back to the tent just before the service started. I was in my trailer. Brother Martin walked in crying and told me about it. "Brother Schambach, she's going to be the first one over the ramp. You're going to lay hands on her on this children's blessing night, and she'll be the first one healed."

"That's exactly right," I said.

You know, I think that little Elisha is the reason that I was sent to that town in the first place. The second I laid hands on her that night, she began to recover. Praise God! As they were driving home that night, Elisha drank a whole bottle in three minutes, which she hadn't done in four whole days. The rattle in her breathing was gone as well.

The next morning they went back to the same doctors. Within a short period of time, they all agreed that her heart was normal. There was no leakage in any of her heart's chambers. She was totally healed! Once again, the doctors were astounded.

In the service that Wednesday night, Elisha walked across the platform smiling and waving to the people.

After four weeks they returned again to the doctor, who congratulated them and told them that she would be off all medication for the rest of her life.

CHAPTER 35

A Blood Transfusion from Calvary

Another child I saw healed was Jonathan Gregori. But this one hit a little closer to home. Jonathan is the son of my niece, Joann. I know that many of you reading this book have loved ones who need a healing touch from God. Well, we preachers are no different. Sometimes we have great needs within our own families.

At age three, Jonathan came down with a blood disease—I.T.P. The platelets in his blood were being destroyed, and within a 24-hour period, there were black and blue bruises all over his body.

His parents didn't know what was happening to him so they took him to the doctor. This particular doctor, when he examined Jonathan, just blurted out, "Oh, your son has leukemia." This devastated Jonathan's parents.

It wasn't long before the boy was in the hospital and was put on heavy medication. They had to pad his crib because the disease caused him to bruise very easily.

It was during that time that I brought the big Gospel tent into that area of the Bronx, New York. One night we had a children's blessing service. My main emphasis that night was healing. And I'll never forget Jonathan's father, Pastor Mark Gregori, bringing him up to the front to be prayed for.

I took the boy from his father's arms and held him. Then I prayed over him, "Give him a blood transfusion from Calvary! In Jesus' name."

Within that same week, Jonathan's platelets came to the right level. The disease was gone! There were no more bruises. He was made completely whole!

Jonathan is a grown man now, and God's using him in His service. He has traveled to several other countries as a missionary. He is a marvelous example of God's healing power that is still at work today.

CHAPTER 36

Ginger Stands Proxy

In an earlier chapter I talked about 'proxy'—standing in the place of someone else and agreeing for God to touch them. That can be for a loved one to get saved, like in the "Broken Needles" story. But it can also be for a loved one's healing. You can read such a story in John's gospel, when Jesus healed the nobleman's son:

So Jesus came again to Cana of Galilee where He had made the water wine. And there was a certain nobleman whose son was sick at Capernaum. When he heard that Jesus had come out of Judea into Galilee, he went to Him and implored Him to come down and heal his son, for he was at the point of death. Then Jesus said to him, "Unless you people see signs and wonders, you will by no means believe." The nobleman said to Him, "Sir, come down before my child dies!" Jesus said to him, "Go your way; your son lives." So the man believed the word that Jesus spoke to him, and he went his way. And as he was now going down, his servants met him and told him, saying, "Your son lives!" Then he inquired of them the hour when he got better. And they said to him, "Yesterday at the seventh hour the fever left him." So the father knew that it was at the same hour in which Jesus said to him, *"Your son lives."* And he himself believed, and his whole household (John 4:46-53).

What an unusual story! Jesus came back to the very area where he turned the water into wine, and a certain man came to Him. This is proxy. He came to stand proxy for his son, who was home, six to nine hours away.

He came to Jesus saying, "Sir, my boy's at the point of death. Come along home with me and heal him."

(Ah, everybody would like to take Him home with them!)

Jesus gave him a gentle rebuke and said, "Unless you see signs and wonders, you will not believe." At another time Jesus said, *"Blessed are those who have not seen and yet have believed"* (John 20:29).

Jesus says the same to you and me today! We don't have to see it to believe it. All we've got to do is hear what the Word of God has to say about it and stand on that Word, and God will bring it to pass. Hallelujah!

After Jesus gave His rebuke, He said to the man, "Your son lives." He didn't go home with him. All He did was speak the word, and the man believed what Jesus spoke to him. So he went his way.

Now here is where the devil likes to gain advantage. When you leave the presence of God and you go home to a boy who's dying, all kinds of thoughts go through your mind. "You're too late! Your boy is gonna die!" You lying devil! I believe what Jesus said. I believe that my son lives!

When that man got home, he found his little boy totally healed. This is a great example of standing proxy for someone else. I've seen God do many outstanding miracles by proxy.

A woman named Ginger put this thing to work.

In 1998, I held a crusade in Newark, New Jersey. I announced to the people that I was going to have "proxy night."

I said, "If you have a loved one in a hospital, you come on proxy night and pray for them, and they're going to be healed."

Ginger heard the word that I spoke. Her sister Kathy had been critically injured in a motorcycle accident. She was in a semi-comatose state known as post-traumatic amnesia and wasn't expected to live. She had terrible brain damage. The look of death was all over her.

The doctors told Ginger that if her sister ever woke up from the coma, that she would be incapacitated. They said she'd never walk, talk, read, or write again. They said she would not remember who anyone was.

But thank God, Ginger did not believe the report of the doctors. She believed the report of the Lord. She took me up on my challenge. When proxy night came, she came ready to agree for her sister.

As I preached that night, the anointing of God was all over the tent. Jesus showed up! Hallelujah! And I told the people, "You've got to tell the Lord what you want!"

You see, I believe that when we pray, we should tell the Lord exactly what we want. We can't just sit back and say, "Well, I'll take whatever the Lord wants to give me." We've got to tell God exactly what we want.

When I said this, Ginger thought about Kathy.

I want my sister back! she thought.

I called people up to walk across the ramp for prayer. Before we even got a chance to lay hands on her, she fell out under the power of God.

Her faith was strong. She believed the report of the Lord and was convinced that her sister was healed. Now, this miracle didn't take place at that exact moment, like when Jesus prayed for the nobleman's son. He had something else in mind that would absolutely blow the mind of the doctor.

Ginger went back to this doctor, whose name was Eileen.

157

"Look, Ginger, I'd love to tell you that they just snap out of it. I'd love to tell you they just get better—like I'll walk down the hall and she'll just be sitting there saying, 'Hey, Eileen. How are you doing?' It just doesn't happen."

But all the time, Ginger was sitting there thinking, *Oh, yes it does. Yes it does.*

So the next day, this doctor was walking down the halls of the ward. As she walked past Kathy's room, she heard a voice.

"Hey, Eileen. How are you doing?" she said. That girl was out of a coma, totally healed and restored by the power of God. I don't know what that Dr. Eileen did after that, but I know that she couldn't deny the power of God.

That's what proxy is all about. We can be in perfect agreement regarding the promises of God, exercise our faith, and watch God work!

CHAPTER 37

Miracle Candy

One night in Philadelphia, a lady came to me and gave me some candy to wear. You can tell by looking at me that I like candy. So I accepted it and thanked her for it. She said, "That isn't for you."

"Well," I said, "you just gave it to me."

She said, "I want you to wear it."

I said, "Hold it, girl. I don't wear candy. I eat candy. What is wrong with you?"

She said, "Why, Brother Schambach, you are going to wear that candy while you preach."

Did you ever run into a stubborn woman? There are a lot of women who will never take no for an answer—they are going to press through and get what God has promised them. This was one of those ladies. She said, "You are going to wear that candy."

I said, "No, I am not going to wear it, woman. What is wrong with you? Other preachers already talk about me wearing cloth. If they find out I am wearing candy, my name is mud."

She said, "Brother 'Mud,' you are going to wear that candy."

She was very persistent. I said, "I am not going to wear it." I just withdrew myself from it. I said, "Why don't you make it a cloth like everybody else does? I will give you a cloth—take my hanky!"

"No, I don't want it," she said. "You are going to wear this candy. I have cloths from your office. I have them from Oral Roberts. I have them from T.L. Osborn. I have a sister in a mental institution. She has been there for 30 years. I send her cloths, but they censor her mail, and they know what those cloths are. The cloths end up in the wastebasket. I just came from there and they told me I can send candy to my sister. Now, you and I are going to put one over on the devil. We are going to cast him out with that candy."

I looked at her and said, "Give me the candy!" I put it in my left hip pocket and started preaching. I returned it to her at the end of the service. "You send it to your sister," I told her.

Six months later, I came back to that city, and I was preaching in the Metropolitan Opera House. I was receiving the offering that night when I saw two ladies come in. To be perfectly honest with you, I didn't remember the woman with the candy. She came walking down the aisle and dropped her offering in the basket and said, "Praise the Lord, Brother Schambach."

I said, "Praise the Lord."

She said, "This is my sister."

I said, "Hi, sister, glad to have you in church."

She said, "Brother Schambach, this is my sister."

So I dropped the bucket, got her by the hand, and said, "Welcome to our crusade." I didn't want to offend her.

She said, "Brother Schambach, do you remember who I am?"

I said, "No, ma'am, I am sorry I don't."

She said, "I am the one who gave you the candy!"

I stopped the offering collection and said, "Everybody go sit down. Forget the offering. I want to hear this."

I didn't get to preach that night. That woman tore the place apart. She told the story that I just told you. Then she said, "I sent that candy to the hospital, and the moment my sister bit into the candy, she bit into the power of God. The demons came out of her instantly, and she was in her right mind for the first time in 30 years."

The hospital staff didn't call the sister for about two weeks. Can you imagine that telephone call? "Come and get your sister."

"What do you mean, come and get her. Is she dead?"

"No! She isn't dead!"

"Well, what is wrong?"

"We don't know. All we know is that for the last two weeks, we have put her through a series of tests. She has been examined by every psychiatrist and every psychologist who had anything to do with her case. For the first time in 30 years, your sister is in her right mind."

What a miracle! This woman started attending a church in Philadelphia that used to be pastored by my brother-in-law, Rev. Harry Donald. She went on to live a normal life and was able to work because her sister didn't give up!

But the preacher almost cost her the miracle… "I am not going to wear that candy!" I learned my lesson that night!

CHAPTER 38

A Miracle in Progress

Not every miracle happens instantaneously. Some miracles are progressive. They don't happen all at once.

I saw this first-hand in Canada, when I put my tent up on the Indian reservation in Hobbema, Alberta.

There was a 17-year-old girl in the audience named Billie Dee Sharmon. The doctors had told her she had all kinds of sicknesses. She could barely move, and didn't go to school for three months. God delivered her from these infirmities there at the tent service.

But there was one thing left that God had not healed, and she came back to the tent the next night ready to receive this final miracle.

When I had my testimony time before the message, she and her mother came across the platform and told the people how God had healed her. I was thrilled to hear the testimony.

But before they left the platform, they had another request from God.

She had lost a lot of her vision because of the sickness. She was going blind. When she was healed, part of it had been restored. But she was believing God for all of it to be restored. They told me this right there on the platform. That's faith!

So I looked at them and said, "You don't have to wait for that. We can pray right now. Right here on television."

You see, I broadcast this message on television. Some preachers might be nervous about everybody watching them pray for the sick. But I love to demonstrate the power of the Gospel. I like to show it, to put it on display!

I had my daughter, Donna, and another pastor join me to pray for her. We ganged up on the devil. I took her glasses off and got ready to pray. But I only got one word out!

"Father—"

Immediately, I felt the power of God on that ramp. And so did she! As we had our hands on her, she just flopped like an old dishrag. It was the anointing of the Holy Ghost!

"Give her 20/20 vision! In the name of Jesus," I prayed.

I knew she wouldn't be able to talk in that state, so I had them take her off the platform.

A little later in the service, Donna came running up to me with the news that the young girl had clear vision! So we brought her back up to see what the Lord had done.

I did a little test to see how clear her vision was, and sure enough, her eyes were totally restored. She didn't need those glasses anymore.

Hallelujah! It was a progressive miracle. God worked on her a little bit at a time, but He completed His work there in that anointing-charged atmosphere, right in front of the television cameras!

CHAPTER 39

An Unexpected Twist

God moves in mysterious ways. Sometimes He does things that do not make sense to the natural mind. When we are being led by His Spirit, sometimes we have to step out in faith and do things that do not make sense to the natural mind.

Throughout my years of ministry, I've been led to do things that must have seemed crazy to the people around me. But if the Holy Ghost tells me to do something, I'm going to do it. I don't care what people think. That's their business. It's my job to be obedient to God and step out in faith. He'll do the rest.

I'll never forget one particular miracle God performed for a woman named Esther Bake. After many years of pain and suffering, He totally healed and restored her. But this miracle required me to do something a little unexpected.

In 1960, Esther had been involved in two automobile accidents. In the first accident, she received a fractured skull, brain damage, and a severe injury to her left leg. Not long after that, she had another accident.

This time, her neck was broken in two places and her spine was chipped all the way down.

After being X-rayed seven times, she was put in traction with sandbags on either side of her head. The orthopedic specialist put her on the critical list, giving her only 72 hours to live. She did survive, but was put in a steel neck brace.

Four years after the accidents, Esther started having severe headaches and eventually went into a coma. She was admitted once again into the hospital, where the doctors found a tumor in her brain. All seemed hopeless. During one night, she felt her spirit leave her body and was looking down at herself from above the room.

A minister came and prayed for her, though, and she did not die. That night, she came out of the coma and felt something draining down her throat. She knew she had been healed, and sure enough, when the doctors re-examined her, the tumor was gone!

But her pain remained. She took pain pills all day so she could sleep at night. Her medical bill alone was $100 a month! This was back in the '60s. That was a lot of money back then.

On July 5, 1971, 11 years after the accidents, Esther stumbled across the Voice of Power radio broadcast. As she heard the Word of God come forth, faith came alive in her heart, and she was determined to get to one of my meetings, believing that the Lord would heal her body.

That year, the day after Thanksgiving, we put the tent up in Miami, close to where Esther lived. I'll never forget seeing her that day in that steel neck brace. She couldn't even turn her head and had to turn her whole body to look around. But her faith was strong.

I called her down to the front.

"What did you come for?"

"I've come for a miracle," she replied.

"Then what are you doing with that steel brace on your neck? Take it off."

Now, I had a lot of guts. Under the unction of the Holy Ghost, I put my hands on her head and said, "In the name of Jesus!"

Then I twisted her head! The entire audience really lost it. Quite frankly, when I look back on the incident, I get a little frightened. No one should ever do that unless the Holy Ghost explicitly directs that way!

To everyone's astonishment, Esther was totally healed! She started moving around more than she had in years. Glory to God!

She went back to her clinic and had the doctors X-ray her. They couldn't even find the break in her neck. Hallelujah! It was gone!

Esther came to me later with a proposition. "Brother Schambach, since God healed me, I want to give Him that $100 a month that I've been spending on medicine."

I said, "No, Esther, you don't want to do that. You've been doing without all these years. Go buy yourself a new wardrobe."

But she insisted. "I want to give it to God," she said.

"Well, okay," I said. After all, I didn't want to rob her of a blessing. "Where are you working, Esther?"

"I work for the city," she said.

"Are you the boss?"

"No, I'm just one of the girls."

"How would you like to run the place?"

Then I prayed for her. Some time after, I put my tent up in South Bay, Florida, where she came to me with another testimony.

"Brother Schambach, they elevated me! Now I am in charge of the whole office. I also got a $300 a month raise, and I can give God that $100 a month, too."

Isn't that beautiful? It was a total and complete miracle, triggered by the faith of a woman who was bold enough to trust God for the impossible.

CHAPTER 40

My Battle With the Devil

I was on the turnpike, driving from Philadelphia to Chicago. I had plenty of time in the car. I was speaking in tongues, prophesying, and dancing. Have you ever danced while you were driving? It was just me and Jesus in that car. Just me and Jesus, having time together. No one was around to say, "You aren't in the Spirit." Just me and Jesus in that automobile.

I was halfway through Ohio, when all of a sudden a pain struck me in the fifth rib. I doubled over the steering wheel. At that moment, my foot hit the brake.

Ol' Slewfoot was sitting on my shoulder. "Heart trouble," he whispered.

I wondered how he got in the car with all the tongue speaking, prophesying, and shouting. How did that devil get in here?

I pulled over to the shoulder of the road and engaged the devil in a conversation. He asked, "How many people did you bury this week?"

I was doubled over, but I thought of all the funerals I had preached at that week. "Four of them," I said.

"What did they die from?" he asked.

Every time that devil jumps on you, he knows how to mess your faith up—even while you are speaking in tongues. He said, "How many of your brothers have died?"

I said, "There's Ruben, Henry, Charles—four?"

"What did they die from?"

If I had seen a grave, I would have jumped in it. That's how bad it hurt! Then I came to my senses and said, "You filthy, rotten, lying devil. You are a liar. How can I have heart trouble when Jesus lives in there?"

He said, "Still hurts, doesn't it?"

I said, "Let it hurt. I am healed anyway. If God said I am healed, then I am; healing is mine."

I pulled the keys out of the ignition. I locked the car and said, "Slewfoot, wait here. I will be back. If I have heart trouble, I won't see you again. I am going to run down this turnpike, and I am going to jog until I get my second wind." I took off running—until I got my second wind. I felt so good as I was coming back that if I would have seen Mohammed Ali, I believe I could have whipped him right then.

When I got back to the car, I couldn't find the devil anywhere. I said, "Where are you, devil? Where are you? I want you to know, I am healed!"

But the devil was long gone. Only Jesus was there.

But He [Jesus] was wounded for our transgressions, He was bruised for our iniquities; the chastisement for our peace was upon Him, and by His stripes we are healed (Isaiah 53:5).

CHAPTER 41

Conclusion
"Everyone Who Asks"

What outstanding testimonies of God's healing power! But He's not finished yet. He is still healing the sick.

In November of 2001, we held a miracle service right on the campus of my Global Outreach Center—my ministry headquarters. There was a woman in the crowd from Pittsburgh, Pennsylvania, who came all the way down there to get a healing touch from God.

Before I even started preaching, she was out of that wheelchair, walking and praising God. I tell you, folks, when that happened, everybody in the place started shouting. It is such a thrill to see that God is still at work.

What do you have need of? Are you oppressed by a spirit of infirmity? Do you need a healing touch from God? He's waiting to perform the miracle for you. You just have to stand on His promises and believe that He'll do it. *"For everyone who asks receives, and he who seeks finds, and to him who knocks it will be opened"* (Matt. 7:8).

If God says "everybody," He means "everybody"!

The devil may be attacking you with infirmity right now. Don't stand for it! You can put the devil where he belongs.

But I want you to know, everything you trust God for, you've got to fight for it. You can't sit in that upholstered pew and say, "Well, whenever the Lord gets ready He's going to drop it in my lap." He isn't going to do anything!

You're going to have to get up and stretch out on His Word and lay some footprints down. You're going to have to eyeball the devil and say, "I've had enough of this!"

Amen! You can put him where he belongs. That devil has no business on your back. He has no business in your head or in your stomach. He has no business in your feet or your legs. He has no business in your chest. There's only one place the devil has any right to be—and that's under your feet! He is a defeated foe!

I want to pray for your healing right now. I don't care what the devil has put on you—God is going to take it off you. So let me pray for your physical condition.

*Father, in Jesus' name, I come against the works of the devil. He's a thief that comes to steal, to kill, and to destroy. But You said you have come that we might have life and have it more abundantly. In the name of Jesus, let resurrection power come alive. Jesus, stretch forth that nail-scarred hand and heal all manner of sickness. I curse blindness and deafness. I curse crippling spirits. I curse heart disease, cancer, back problems, and liver trouble. Satan, I adjure you by Jesus, **loose** your hold on this individual's life. From the crown of their head to the soles of their feet to their fingertips, let that healing power come alive now. In Jesus Christ's name, and by faith I call it done. Amen and amen.*

Now rejoice and give God praise for what He's done!

Some of you are in the hospital. Get up out of that bed that you're lying in. In the name of Jesus, I say unto you, arise! Arise and be healed! Be delivered and be set free. The devil is a liar. Don't listen to him. You're going to rise and be healed! Go ahead! Do something you haven't done before. Let the devil know you're not putting up with his sickness anymore. You're healed! You're healed! You're healed!

PART IV

FINANCIAL *Miracles*

"You Can't Beat God Givin'"

God is the best giver in the world. That's what this book is going to show you: how God continually gives to those who obey Him, because you can't beat God giving! I remember the sawdust on the ground at the old tent services and the mamas and the little grandmas who would march up the trail to the altar with their offerings to God, singing:

> *You can't beat God givin' no matter how you try*
> *You can't beat God givin' no matter how you try*
> *The more you give, the more He gives you*
> *Just keep on givin' because it's really true*
> *You can't beat God givin' no matter how you try*

But you know, these are more than just the words to a beautiful song. This is a tried and true principle of God's Word. The people you are going to read about are people just like you and me, people who heard the voice of God, obeyed Him, and were richly blessed for it. They are people like the little widow of Zarephath in 1 Kings 17. Do you remember her story?

God was angry at the wickedness of the people of Israel because their queen, Jezebel, had made Baal the idol in their land. God had anointed Elijah and told him to let Jezebel know there was going to be a great famine in their land because she wouldn't repent and lead the people back to God. The famine started, and it was terrible: no rain, dead crops. People began to starve to death. It was all right for Elijah for a little while because God led him to a nice babbling brook where he could relax all day, and every evening eat food God sent ravens to give him. But one day that brook dried up because there wasn't any rain. The ravens were more than a little late coming that day. They didn't show up at all. God said, "Go over to Zarephath; I have a widow lady there who's going to take care of you."

This idea probably didn't seem too good to Elijah. In the first place, Queen Jezebel wasn't too happy with him right then; in fact, she was looking everywhere for him because she figured he was responsible for the famine that was ruining their land. And Zarephath was the queen's hometown. God might as well have been saying, "Put your head in the lion's mouth." In the second place, widow ladies in the Bible times weren't known for having a lot of means to support starving prophets. If a widow didn't have a grown-up son to provide for her, she was pretty likely to starve to death—especially in the middle of a famine!

But Elijah did what God commanded. Look in 1 Kings 17.

> *And the word of the Lord came unto him, saying, Arise, get thee to Zarephath, which belongeth to Zidon, and dwell there: behold, I have commanded a widow woman there to sustain thee.*
>
> *So he arose and went to Zarephath. And when he came to the gate of the city, behold, the widow woman was there gathering of sticks: and he called to her, and said, Fetch me, I pray three, a little water in a vessel, that I may drink.*
>
> *And as she was going to fetch it, he called to her, and said, Bring me, I pray thee, a morsel of bread in thine hand.*

And she said, As the Lord thy God liveth, I have not a cake, but an handful of meal in a barrel, and a little oil in a cruse: and, behold, I am gathering two sticks, that I may go in and dress it for me and my son, that we may eat it, and die.

And Elijah said unto her, Fear not; go and do as thou hast said: but make me thereof a little cake first, and bring it unto me, and after make for thee and for thy son.

For thus saith the Lord God of Israel, The barrel of meal shall not waste, neither shall the cruse of oil fail, until the day that the Lord sendeth rain upon the earth.

And she went and did according to the saying of Elijah: and she, and he, and her house, did eat many days.

And the barrel of meal wasted not, neither did the cruse of oil fail, according to the word of the Lord, which he spake by Elijah (1 Kings 17:8-16 KJV).

Can you see this picture? When the prophet came to the gates of Zarephath, he saw a skinny, broken-down little widow woman picking up sticks. "Praise the Lord, sister," he said to her. "I sure am thirsty. Will you go get me a drink?"

She said, "Praise the Lord, brother. I'll get you a drink right now."

But then Elijah said, "Wait a minute. Will you bring me a morsel of bread, too?"

This little lady, with a stricken look on her face, told the prophet, "As the Lord liveth, I don't have any bread. Haven't you heard about the famine?" (*If she only knew he was the rascal who caused the famine!*)

"I'm down to my *last* cake, and I'm out here picking up sticks for the *last* time. I'm going to mix the meal for the *last* time and strike the fire for the *last* time; then, my son and I are going to sit down to a meal together for the *last* time."

Everything was last, last, last. This lady thought this was her last day on earth because she and her boy were going to starve to death after they finished this little bit of meal.

How do you think this made Elijah feel knowing that God thought this starving little widow was going to take care of him?

But I'll let you in on a secret: God doesn't look at things the same way we do. What looks like nothing to us is something to God. God is the Creator. He can make something out of our nothing. That's why many times, when you are waiting for God to do something in your life—to give you something or to change a situation in your life, when you need a real touch from Him—He just waits. He waits until you are down to "nothing"; because that's exactly when God can do His biggest miracles—God can do something great with your "nothing." But it takes obedience to clear the way for God to do a miracle!

I know a lot of preachers who pray, "Lord, just send a millionaire to my church. Send me a millionaire." But that's probably not going to happen. Elijah might have been praying, "Lord, make this widow lady of Zarephath a very rich widow"; but no, God sent Elijah to a little lady who was about to starve to death. God doesn't need to work through millionaires and rich widows; He can work through people like that little lady of Zarephath.

That little widow didn't have enough food to feed a hungry prophet like Elijah; she had her own child to feed. But Elijah told her, "You go do just what you said—make that last bit of bread—but give it to me, and then feed you and your son."

You see, preachers have always had a lot of nerve, even back in Bible times! Elijah, who had been waiting on ravens to bring him food, had a lot of nerve asking this woman to give him her last meal.

But that widow lady knew Elijah was a man of God, and God had already spoken to her and told her to step out on faith and give what she had to the man of God.

If God speaks to you, He expects you to listen. Even if you're down to your very last dollar, if God says to give it to His Church, you had better listen. He doesn't ask you to give something unless He has something bigger and better planned for you.

The widow of Zarephath went in and mixed up her last little cake and gave it to Elijah. Then she mixed up a cake for her son and a cake for her. And the Bible says there was more meal and more oil, and that the meal barrel wasted not for more than 1,000 days. That's over three years! For three years that lady had a perpetual miracle right in her home because she obeyed the voice of God.

I can just hear her, "Brother, you can stay right here with me in Zarephath. You don't need to go down the street to Sister Jones' house. She hasn't got a thing to eat down there. You stay here, and I'll take care of you." And for three years, until that famine ended, they ate and drank and were fine in her house.

Now, a lot of people say to me, "Brother Schambach, these are the worst economic times I can remember in years. I can barely make the house payment, and I just can't afford to give an offering until things start looking up. I haven't even been tithing."

And I always say to those people, "You are making the biggest mistake that you could possibly make. A time of calamity, a time of poverty, or a time of disaster is the very worst time to stop giving. Can you think of a worse calamity than the one facing the little widow of Zarephath? She and her son had been surviving by sharing one little cake every day, until finally they were down to the very last cake. She had no business at all giving that cake to someone else! That was the very worst day of her life. She had nothing to share. But what would have happened to her and her son if she had told the man of God, "You know, I just can't afford to give until things start looking up"? Both she and her boy would have perished. Instead, because she was obedient and gave even in the midst of terrible need, she received a perpetual miracle of abundant food for three years.

All around her was famine; thousands of people were starving to death, but because Elijah and the widow obeyed God, the famine did not touch them at all. So although there may be difficult economic times, and all around you people may be in dire circumstances, God is not going to let that touch you if you are obedient to Him.

Here is a promise from God for you:

You shall not be afraid of the terror by night, nor of the arrow that flies by day, Nor of the pestilence that walks in darkness, nor of the destruction that lays waste at noonday. A thousand may fall at your side, And ten thousand at your right hand; But it shall not come near you (Psalm 91:5-7).

You don't have to worry about the recession or the economy. Whatever is happening to the rest of the world doesn't have to touch you. All you have to do is obey the voice of God.

There was a famine in the land, and all the widow's neighbors were starving and dying, but she didn't pay attention to that; she simply took God at His Word. She gave one little meal cake, and God gave back to her a thousand times over what she had given. You just can't beat God giving!

I'm not saying that if you give your last dollar today to God's work that you're going to get rich, because I don't believe God makes petty deals like that. But I will tell you this: *God honors our giving.*

We have God's promise.

But this I say: He who sows sparingly will also reap sparingly, and he who sows bountifully will also reap bountifully. So let each one give as he purposes in his heart, not grudgingly or of necessity; for God loves a cheerful giver. And God is able to make all grace abound toward you, that you, always having all sufficiency in all things, may have an abundance for good work (2 Corinthians 9:6-8).

In my work and ministry, I have met hundreds of people and heard hundreds of stories of God's children obeying His voice and receiving in return the very desires of their heart. You're going to meet some of those people in the pages of this book, and I know that it is going to bless and inspire you.

Be encouraged. Your back may be up against the wall right now financially. You're about to read some more stories of people who had their backs against the wall, but they stepped out in faith, believing that God would provide. As you read their testimonies, let faith stir in your heart, and know that God wants to do the same thing for you.

CHAPTER 42

God Provides Food

My mama was a woman of faith. Mama had twelve children, and six of us were at home. When you're trusting God for six kids, it takes some faith. Pop was laid off from the railroad. When it was time for supper, Mom never asked you what you wanted. We never asked what it was; we were just glad to get it. We all had our same spot around the table. One time she called us out for supper. My place was next to the oven. Jim sat next to me; Leroy on the other side—he was bigger. I felt that oven, and it was cold. I nudged Jim. I looked down at the dishes, and they were empty. But Mom had called us here to eat.

My mother was a woman of God! She sat us kids around that table, and she said, "All right, now, quiet. We are going to pray and thank God for the food."

I nudged Jim again. I said, "Mom flipped her wig. 'Thank God for the food'? There isn't any food."

She was oblivious to natural surroundings. Anybody can thank God for a hot dog in his hand. You can thank God for food in your refrigerator. But she was thanking God for nothing. She started to pray. "Lord, in Jesus' name, bless all the missionaries who don't have anything."

I nudged Jim again. "We're missionaries. We don't have anything."

But Mama went right on. "Lord, we thank You for what You have provided."

My one eye came open. I thought that mashed potato dish was going to fill up right on the spot. I thought that meat plate was going to have meat on it. Still nothing was there. Mom was still thanking God for it. She said, "Lord, You have never failed me. The Lord will provide. I thank You for taking care of my family."

Inside I was saying, *I wish she would hurry up. I know somebody who has some food. I'll go up there and get some as soon as she gets done.* As soon as she said, "Amen," our back door opened. In popped Sister Landis with two chickens already stuffed and cooked. Then in came a man with a jug of milk and two loaves of homemade bread.

I nudged Jim again. "Hey! Mom got it, boy! Mom knows what she's talking about."

I'm talking about a prevailing kind of faith that holds on to the horns of the altar (see 1 Kings 1:50-51). Don't give up! Thank God for it. The answer is on the way. Get your eyes off that situation. Get your eyes off that trouble in your family relationship. Get your eyes off the balance in your checkbook. Get your eyes on the promise. If God said it, He will do it. He will not have His seed begging bread. You are a child of God. He will make a way where there is no way. Hang on to the horns of the altar until that answer gets here.

CHAPTER 43

The Back Rent Blues

One night, at a crusade meeting, a lady walked down the aisle of the big auditorium. Tears were streaming down her face. She was holding a long sheet of paper.

There were 1,500 to 2,000 people in the audience, and everybody was being blessed but her. She was weeping desperately, grieving so deeply that it kind of grew over the whole congregation.

She said, "Brother Schambach, they are going to put me out of my house. I am four months behind in my rent." She held up the paper. "This is a notice of eviction. Tomorrow morning at ten o'clock, they are going to move everything out to the sidewalk."

I jumped off that platform and said, "Woman, the devil is a liar. They are not putting you out on the sidewalk. You are a child of God."

She said, "What about this notice?"

I took it, tore it up, and threw it under the platform. "That is your problem. You are looking at the circumstances. If you continue to do that, you will not have faith. You have to start looking in the Bible.

And my God shall supply all your need according to His riches in glory by Christ Jesus (Philippians 4:19).

The reason sick people can't get healed is that they are too busy looking at their diseases. The more they look at them, the worse they feel. We need to keep our eyes on the Word.

I did my best to encourage this woman's faith. She was weeping vehemently.

She said, "Brother Schambach, my blind mama lives with me, and all I can see is my blind mother sitting on the step."

I said, "Shut up! You are getting to me now, woman!" (*I guess that is why I am not pastoring anymore.*) The devil is not going to put you out on the sidewalk. Sit down in that front row and listen to me preach."

I have never seen such anxiety in an individual. I had a sermon prepared but didn't use it. I left all those people, jumped down to where she was, and I preached to that woman for a solid hour. She needed it. I didn't even receive the offering until I finished preaching. Then, when I finished preaching, I went to her and said, "It is time to receive the offering."

She almost fainted. She looked up at me and said, "Don't you remember me? I need money."

I said, "I know it. Where is your pocketbook?"

She said, "But I need—"

I knew she needed money. I am a good listener. She told me she was four months behind in the rent. She also said, "I gave the man $50, but he threw it back at me because it wasn't nearly enough." I had heard that part. I knew she had $50.

I asked, "Where is your purse?"

She said, "Mama has it." Her blind mother was in the service.

I said, "Get it. You are going to give something to God."

She got mad at me. You can tell when folks get mad. But I stayed sweet because I knew she was going to be glad all over again. I was showing her the way to deliverance, and she didn't know it. I said, "We don't have much time. It is ten o'clock at night. At ten o'clock in the morning, they are coming to evict you. You do what I tell you to do, woman."

I could have taken the money out of the church treasury, and I could have paid her rent. But then she would have owed it to God, because that is God's money.

I thought, "Why not just put your faith to work and let her receive a blessing? When God blesses her with it, she will have to pay the tithe and everyone will be blessed." This is how God works!

The woman got up in a huff and went to the back to get her purse. I saw her coming and turned my back to her as I was holding the bucket. I didn't know whether she was going to hit me with her purse or what. I didn't even want to see what she put in.

But I had challenged her to give, and she gave. When it came time for prayer, I said, "I want your blind mama first in that line." Her blind mother was indeed the first in line. I said to the woman, "Stand behind her." Then, I called the prayer line. I laid hands on 500 or 600 people that night, including the blind woman. I rebuked the blind spirit. Her eyes didn't come open suddenly. Sometimes God does it suddenly, instantly, immediately—but sometimes the healing is gradual. Yet in my spirit, I knew God had healed her.

I told her, "Mother, will you do what I tell you to do?"

She said, "Anything you say, I will do it." What a difference between her and her daughter.

I said, "Mama, I want you to go home tonight saying nothing but 'Thank You, Jesus, for giving me 20/20 vision.' Keep thanking Him until your head hits the pillow. You will wake up with perfect sight."

She said, "I will do it." She started down the ramp and said, "Devil, you are a liar. I am not blind anymore. I am thanking Jesus for 20/20 vision."

I said, "Go ahead, Mama, the whole way home."

Then it was time to pray for the woman. I laid hands on her also. I prayed a very simple prayer. I said, "Lord, I don't know how You are going to do this." I don't know how He heals folks either. All I know is He does it. So I prayed, "I am asking You to perform a miracle and pay this woman's debt." Then I said to the woman, "Look at me. In the name of Jesus, I command you to go home and unpack all those bags."

She said, "How do you know I have my bags packed?"

I said, "The way you are talking, I am surprised you haven't moved."

She said, "Half of it is at my brother's house."

"Well, get it back," I answered. "You aren't going anywhere."

That was a Sunday night. On Monday night, I was getting ready to preach when the back door of the church bounced open. This woman wasn't walking in—she was floating in. She was six feet in the air! She was halfway down the aisle when I stopped her.

"Don't you remember me?" she asked.

I said, "I know who you are. But I am not passing up this opportunity for a sermon. I want to ask you one question. Why didn't you come to church like that last night?"

We let our troubles get to us.

I said, "The way you came into this building tonight is the way you ought to come to church no matter what kind of trouble you are going through. Psalm 100:4 says, 'Enter into His gates with thanksgiving, And into His courts with praise. Be thankful to Him, and bless His name.' I can tell by looking at you that God did something. Come down here."

She said, "This morning, I was awakened by the smell of coffee brewing, bacon frying, and homemade biscuits baking. I sat up in my bed, catching the aroma of this breakfast. I looked over into my blind mama's bed, and it was empty. I quickly threw on a robe and ran out into the kitchen. There was my mama making breakfast. She has been blind for 16 years, brother."

She said, "Mama, what are you doing?"

Her mother said, "Brother Schambach told me I would wake up seeing this morning, and the man of God was right. You have been making my breakfast all these years. I thought I would give you the best breakfast you ever had, daughter."

The daughter said, "We didn't eat breakfast. We had church in the kitchen at eight o'clock in the morning. At ten o'clock the constable was supposed to be there. I looked up and said, 'Oh, God, if You can open Mama's eyes, You can pay the rent. Take Your time. You still have two hours.'"

That is what I call faith. I don't know whether I could have said that with only two hours left, but when God does something for you personally, you can trust Him for the next hurdle.

At 8:30 the mailman came. She thought, *Maybe this is the way God is going to do it.* She picked up and opened the six letters she had received. You know how you open the mail looking for money? But there was no money—instead she got bills! Isn't that just like the devil? Now that her faith was strong and she was trusting God for money, she got four bills. But she just laid them on the table and said, "Lord, while You are paying the rent, please catch these four bills too!"

It was nine o'clock. The phone rang. It was a call from a woman whose name she didn't even remember.

"Well, you should remember me," the lady said. "Fourteen or fifteen years ago, you loaned me some money."

"Yeah! Now I remember you." But she never thought she would get that money back.

The lady said, "Honey, I know you thought I would never pay you back. But last night something got a hold of me." The woman explained that she had been in Chicago, shopping, when an overwhelming power took hold of her and seemed to push her toward State Street. She found herself at Pacific Garden Mission, the famous ministry where Billy Sunday got saved. I have visited that place many times. It is still open, and many people get saved in that mission. But this lady had never been to a mission in her life. The Holy Ghost dragged her in, and she sat in the back seat. A man stood up behind the rostrum to give his sermon. At the close, he gave an altar call. The lady got up. The same power that had dragged her down State Street also dragged her down that aisle. She was on her knees getting saved at the altar.

This is the best part of the story as far as I am concerned. That woman not only got saved, but as she knelt there, she got a second blessing. She heard the voice of God. God said to her, "Do you remember the woman who let you borrow money 14 years ago?"

She said, "Yes, Lord, I do remember."

God said, "I want you to pay it back. Restitution is what it is called, wherever possible."

She said, "Well, Lord, I will find out where she lives, and I will send her a check."

God said, "No check. She needs the cash, and I not only want you to pay what you owe her but also give her six percent interest for 14 years." God is a just God, isn't He?

She said, "But Lord, I don't know how to get in touch with her."

God told her the phone number! God even knows your telephone number. He knows your deadline—and where to find you in time to meet it. He said, "She needs it by ten o'clock in the morning."

192

The lady who was about to be evicted went to her old friend's house, got her money, and got back a few minutes before ten o'clock. The constable was there. She put four months' back rent on the table and four months in advance. The constable tore up the notice to evict.

When the lady finished her story, I just had one question for her: "Aren't you glad you trusted God?"

Hallelujah! You don't have any trouble. All you need is faith in God!

CHAPTER 44

Obedience Pays Off

Many years ago, I bought a theater in Brooklyn, New York. Back then, I couldn't get churches to sponsor my meetings. I was too radical. We got so many people saved, I had to buy my own building and start a church, because I surely couldn't send them to those cold, dead churches.

So I went there to raise money for the thing. If I stayed ten days, surely I could get the down payment for the building.

There was a man who desperately needed a new truck. He was driving an old piece of junk. Have you ever driven one of those things? You've got to lay hands on it before it starts, and then you have to lay hands on it to make it stop!

The first night, this man came walking down the aisle. He said, "Brother Schambach, God spoke to me."

I said, "What did God tell you to do, brother?"

"Well, I've been saving for a new truck," he said. "But every time I save, another emergency comes, and I've got to dip into that fund.

Now, I have some money here that I've been saving for that truck. While you were praying, the Lord spoke to me."

"Tell me what He said, brother," I pleaded.

"Well, I've got $500 in my pocket," he said. "And God told me if I gave Him that $500, He'll give me a new truck."

I said, "Who told you that?"

"God did," he replied.

"Well, get your money out! You can't buy a new truck anywhere for $500. If God said He'll do it, He's going to do it!"

First of all, God wants you to be obedient. I want to encourage you in your own finances that God wants to bless you—everything that your hands touch. But you've got to be obedient to the word of the Lord.

So, that man turned the money loose.

The next night he came in there with an envelope that was so big it could have choked an elephant! I mean, it was huge. That's because there were 26 $100 bills inside.

"Oh, brother," I said, "there must be a story here!"

So I gave him the microphone and he told us one of the craziest stories I've ever heard in my life!

He was driving that old wreck of a truck down the streets of Brooklyn, and God spoke to him and said, "Stop the truck! Get out of the truck and lift up the hood."

When he did, God said, "Look down by the carburetor."

Now, God wouldn't talk to me like that, because if He asked me to look for the carburetor, I'd open the trunk. I don't know where it is. I'm not mechanically inclined. But this man knew where it was.

So the man looked down under the carburetor. He said, "Am I losing my mind? I'm looking, and I don't see anything but a carburetor." So he shut the hood, got back in and started chugging back down the street. But God stopped him again.

"I told you to stop this truck and look down there by the carburetor."

So he stopped the truck and lifted the hood. He said, "Lord, I'm looking."

God said, "Look with your hand."

When he put his hand down by the carburetor, he got a hold of something that didn't belong there. It was a roll the size of an oil filter, all covered with grease. God said, "That's it. Break it off."

He broke it off. Inside that baked grease was $26,000, all in 100-dollar bills. He was able to buy a brand new truck, and had brought me the tithes from the money.

When he told his story, that whole church went wild. They started hollering, screaming and praising God. There were about a half dozen men that got up and ran out. I think they were out there looking under their carburetors!

Praise God! This man gave an offering, and the Lord saw his heart.

When you're in financial need, you think maybe God is going to talk to somebody wealthy to come and give you help. Don't ever wonder how He is going to do it, because God's just going to turn around and do it some other way. He moves in mysterious ways!

Chapter 45

Brother Keith Proves God

Read with me in Mark 12:41-44:

Now Jesus sat opposite the treasury and saw how the people put money into the treasury. And many who were rich put in much. Then one poor widow came and threw in two mites, which make a quadrans. So He called His disciples to Himself and said to them, "Assuredly, I say to you that this poor widow has put in more than all those who have given to the treasury; for they all put in out of their abundance, but she out of her poverty put in all that she had, her whole livelihood."

I love that story! Jesus said that this woman gave more than *all* of the other people who gave to the treasury.

That doesn't make any sense to the natural mind. It would seem that other people gave a lot more money than she did. But God does His own math! All those rich people had plenty to spare. But this precious little woman gave everything she had.

God wants us to lay it all on the line. That's what this woman did, and Jesus took notice.

A brother named Keith illustrated this principle.

I was holding a crusade in Baltimore. Keith and his wife came with some friends to the day service, where they heard my daughter, Donna, preach.

During the service, someone broke into the van they had ridden in. After this, they decided to just go home rather than staying for the evening service.

But then they ran into me. While they were waiting in the lobby of a nearby hotel for the police to arrive and take their report, we crossed paths. I greeted them like I would anybody else.

After we met, God told them to stay for the evening service and hear my message.

Now, Keith and his wife only had a few dollars between them. After paying the parking fee, they had 35 cents each. They were embarrassed to put 35 cents in the offering plate, but it was all they had, so they gave it.

It wasn't only the offering that they were worried about, though. Keith and his wife were heavily invested in their own ministry at the time, a home for troubled girls. They had bills to pay but didn't see how they were going to pay them. God knew. He saw their faith as they put the little they had in the offering.

Keith made a vow to God the next day. He said, "If you bless us with some money today, I'll give what I would like to have given last night. I'll give Brother Schambach $200."

That day, they received a check in the mail for $1,750!

It didn't matter to God that they had hardly any money. What mattered to Him was their faith. He honored that faith when they were obedient to Him.

CHAPTER 46

Power Partner Pennaman

Our ministry has what we call Power Partners. Power Partners not only pray with me, but they also help the ministry financially every month. They give $25 a month, and God blesses them.

I met a black brother in New York, Brother Pennaman. I went to preach at Madison Square Garden, and he sent me a letter. I opened that letter and a $100 check fell out. I opened it again, and a $500 check dropped out. After that I shook it, but that was the end of it, except for one of the most beautiful letters I have ever read. It blessed me.

He told me, "Brother Schambach, ever since you started Power Partners, I wanted to give, but I've been on welfare. You know, when you're on welfare, you just don't have enough money for everything. But I sent you 25 cents a week. That's a dollar a month. God started to bless me. Before long, I could send you $5 a month. You were praying for me, and the folks down there at your office were praying. Then I started sending $10 a month, and finally I became a Power Partner. You sent me that pin and my Bible. Then God got me off welfare."

That's what I desire. I want to get folks off the welfare system. I want God to bless His people. Now you read this story. It will bless your soul. This man said, "Brother Schambach, I started getting blessed. The city gave me a job managing some apartment buildings. I was making so much money that I changed from $25 a month. The blessing of God kept being poured out on me. I had more money than I knew what to do with, so I made it $50 a month."

I mean, he was blessing me now!

He said, "Brother Schambach, now I've got two apartment buildings that I'm managing for the city. I'm sending you $100 a month now. I never made so much money in all my life. This $100 check is my Power Partner pledge for the month. That $500 check—I just got so much I don't know what to do with it. Just put it anywhere you want to."

That's a man who came from the welfare system who couldn't afford to give 25 cents a week!

When you give to God first, and you make a commitment, then God is going to see that you get blessed. When you're paying your tithes, don't give God what's left. A lot of times we take the rent out. Then we pay the phone bill, then the light bill. And we say, "Lord, this is what I have left now. I'm going to give you some."

That's all wrong. No wonder you're messed up. You take God's right off the top. Say, "Lord, this belongs to You. You're first in my life." When you start giving to God what belongs to Him, you're headed for the greatest blessing of your life.

CHAPTER 47

God's Business

Mary Van Lare is another faithful Power Partner with my ministry. She owns a rehabilitation company in Wisconsin. God worked a mighty miracle for her business because she gave sacrificially to Him.

Now, she was no stranger to the miracle-working power of God. She had already seen first-hand what God can do for those who have faith in Him.

One summer, she fractured her knee so badly that the doctor told her she would need a total knee replacement. It was around this time that she was introduced to my ministry.

She listened to a series of my audiotapes in her car. As she listened to those tapes, she let her faith build and build. She found out that I was going to be holding a crusade in her area, so she told her surgeon to wait until after she went to the crusade.

To make a long story short, Jesus healed her knee. She still has the X-rays to prove it!

Years later, she was on a business trip in Arlington, Texas, when two men attacked her in her hotel room. They robbed her and beat her to a pulp. She woke up in the emergency room.

The doctor told her she had a closed head injury, double vision, and that she was badly beaten all over. She wasn't even able to sit on the edge of her bed without falling over. But she was confident that the Lord would heal her.

The normal human reaction would be to hate those men who could do such a thing. But that wasn't Mary's reaction. She forgave them. She prayed for them to get saved.

It was her forgiveness that unlocked the power of God in her life. The next day the double vision was gone. Two days later she could stand. Three days later she could walk. Four days later she was released to go home. God restored her health.

So as you can see, Mary had seen the power of God in action. But we're talking about financial miracles. Well, God did that, too!

Mary's company was the seventh largest woman-owned company in Wisconsin in 1998. But 1999 was a rough year.

They lost a great deal of money in the first six months. They were in a financial tailspin! So do you know what Mary did? She got on her face and cried out to God. She just committed the situation to Him. The Lord reminded her of when she had been attacked by those men. "Mary, just as I sustained you, I will sustain the company."

Mary had already been tithing to Schambach Ministries out of what her company made. But during this time, she promised God that she would start double tithing if He would see them through the year. Well, 85 percent of the rehab companies in the United States went out of business, but the Lord allowed her company to break even.

You may say, "Well, that's not much of a miracle." Just wait. The best part is yet to come!

In January of 2000, the company made more money than it had in the entire 22 1/2 years that it had been in existence! In just one month!

Hallelujah! God blessed Mary because she made her business His business.

CHAPTER 48

The $100 House

Faith was high in Chicago; we were having a great meeting. I took almost a truckload of canes and crutches and wheelchairs out of that meeting. Faith was so high, in fact, that I challenged the 3,500 people in the audience, "I dare you to give God the biggest bill you've got."

I never heard so many groans in all my life. I had 21 preachers on the platform, and they were thinking, *Oh, Lord, I knew I should have changed that 20-dollar bill before I got to church.*

I believe it was one of the greatest offerings I ever received for God. Everybody accepted the challenge. There was one black preacher, a dear friend of mine, who came and stood behind me holding something in his hand. I put the bucket around and said, "Turn it loose, brother."

He said, "Man, you don't know what I've got."

I said, "What have you got?"

He said, "Man, I've got one of those $100 bills."

"It's going to take some faith to turn that thing loose," I told him.

He said, "Well, it ain't mine."

"What's it doing in your hand?" I asked.

"Well," he said, "I got caught speeding. I was fined $100. I was going to pay that fine tomorrow."

I said, "Go pay the fine."

He said, "But I want the blessing!"

I said, "Turn it loose, then."

"What about the fine?"

I said, "Pay it."

"But I want to be blessed."

"You aren't putting me in the middle," I said. "Fight the devil yourself." Meanwhile, people were still coming, putting $20s and $10s in the offering. Finally he came and turned loose of that $100. He watched it float all the way to the bottom of the bucket.

I'll never forget this as long as I live. We continued our meetings for 30 days. They were tremendous meetings in that coliseum in Chicago. The very next night after I received that offering, I heard many testimonies of people who got blessed because they gave, because they had accepted the challenge.

One pastor said, "I had $6. I gave God the $5; I kept the $1. Today God blessed me with $167."

Another person said, "I gave $10 and got $400."

I went to my friend and said, "What did you get back?"

He said, "Nothing."

The second night more people testified. Once again, when I asked my friend what he had received, he said, "Nothing!" He was getting nervous now. The third night I didn't bother asking him; he had his head between his knees moaning, "Oh, Lord." I knew he hadn't received anything. The fourth night he wasn't even there. But on the fifth night, I was getting ready to preach when the back doors opened, and he bounced in. I saw something white in his hand. He had a white piece of paper and he hollered, "Schambach, I got it!"

Inside I was saying, "Lord, it's about time." But to him I said, "Come on, brother, tell us about it."

I didn't get to preach that night. He tore the place up with the story I'm telling you. He said, "This preacher taught me something: that God doesn't always return a blessing in 24 hours. Sometimes you have to wait on Him.

But those who wait on the Lord Shall renew their strength; they shall mount up with wings like eagles, they shall run and not be weary, they shall walk and not faint (Isaiah 40:31).

He went on, "I've been sitting here struggling the last few nights listening to you testify. I gave my best, too. You all got something back, and I was sitting there wondering what was wrong with me. I had given $100. This morning I got a telephone call from a full-gospel businessman in Chicago."

This Christian man had said, "Brother, can you be in my office at one o'clock today? I've got something for you."

My friend said, "Yes, sir, I sure can be there. But where is your office? I don't know who you are."

The businessman said, "Well, I don't know who you are, either, but you be here." So he gave my friend directions to his office.

At one o'clock in that man's office, the businessman said, "God has blessed me in this city over the past 30 years. Before I go to work in the morning, I always pray to get the direction of the Holy Spirit. This morning God told me to give you a house."

My friend stared at the man and said, "But I don't even know you."

The businessman said, "That's what I told God, 'I don't know the man.' God said, 'I do.' God blessed me with a lot of property in this city, and He told me to give you the best house I have." He already had the deed made out to my friend. The deed was for a $50,000 home.

With tears running down his face, my friend told the businessman, "My wife and I have been pastoring here for three years, living in one room with our three children. We've been on the verge of doubting the call of God: Did God really call us? If God called, why do we have to go through this? The other night I was in another preacher's meeting, down to my last $100, and that wasn't even mine. But God worked on me to turn that offering loose. How I thank God now that I turned it loose! I had to be reduced to nothing. But how did you find me, brother? I don't have a telephone listing; you don't know where I live."

The businessman said, "I know. I told the Lord that I didn't know how to get in touch with you; I didn't know where you lived. But God told me your telephone number. God gave me that number when I called you this morning and told you to come to my office."

When my friend finished telling the story, he put the deed to his house into my hand—I saw it; I read it. I was the first one he had shown it to. I would have loved to tell that story that night, but it was his story, and he told it with such joy!

Of course, that night, after the service, everyone wanted to give $100 and get a free house, but I turned around and rebuked them. I said, "Now that you saw somebody put it to work and get a blessing, you want to try it. It isn't going to work the same way for you. You've got to move when God moves or you will be moving on your own."

Do you remember when the children of Israel were at Kadesh-barnea? (See Numbers 13-14.) Two reports came back from the twelve spies sent to search out the Promised Land before the Israelites went in. The reports came back like this: ten spies said, "There's no way we can take this land," and two spies said, "Let's do it in God's name!"

The ten spies were so scared of going into that land, and they frightened the people so much, that the crowd picked up stones to kill Joshua and Caleb, the two faithful spies.

God was so angry about their failure to obey Him and enter into the land that He said, "I'm going to kill every one of them."

But Moses interceded and said, "Don't destroy them, Lord."

God said, "All right, Moses. I won't kill them, but turn them around. They're not going into the land I promised them."

But when the people heard that—and after they had a chance to sleep on it—they came to Moses the next day and said, "We changed our minds. We trust God after all. We want to go claim the land."

But God said, "No, they don't. If they go now, they're going on their own."

When God moves, when you feel the rustling of His Spirit, you had better move with Him or you'll move on your own!

CHAPTER 49

The $600 Tent

One night during a tent revival, I told the folks, "I need 1,000 people across this nation who will give me $100, and this tent will be paid for."

I saw a grown man dressed up nicely, and I could tell that he was a preacher. He was weeping, vehemently sobbing, heading right for me. He had six $100 bills in his hand. He put them in my hand. I said, "What are you crying for, brother?"

"Oh," he said, "I'm an evangelist, and I lost my tent. I've been saving this to buy a tent. And sitting there, God told me to give my tent savings to you!"

I knew what he was going through. But I also knew that when God tells you to make a step of faith, He has a plan and a reward in mind. I said, "Is that all He told you—just to give it?"

And this young evangelist said, "No, sir. He said if I gave it, He was going to give me a tent."

I said, "Then dry the tears up, brother." I took him by the hand, and I prayed for him. I said, "Lord, don't just give him a tent, but give him the chairs that go with it. And while You're doing that, Lord, give him a brand new organ. And while You're doing that, Lord, give him a new truck to carry it in."

The young man wasn't crying anymore. He was saying, "Yeah, Lord! May God answer the man of God's prayer!"

Six months later, that same young evangelist came and grabbed me and danced me around and said, "Thank you preacher! Thank you for taking that money!"

I said, "I'd like to have this on record—somebody thanking me for taking an offering."

He said, "God answered your prayer. God gave me a brand new tent with the chairs, the platform, the Hammond organ, and a brand-new truck, and it didn't cost me a dime. Thank God I obeyed His voice!"

When *you* trust God with an offering, you may not get the same return. But God knows just what you need. He responds to our faith and obedience. When we trust God even in our need, He knows how to open doors we never dreamed possible!

CHAPTER 50

Woman Pledges, God Provides

Not long ago, the Lord placed it on my heart to challenge people to give to God in a special way. He instructed me to tell them to pledge $2,000, and to send the tithe on that, which is $200. The Lord told me that in 90 days, He would provide the other $1,800. After this step of faith, God would set them free from the bondage of debt, and bless them in their finances.

Well, a woman named Doria took me up on that.

In April of 2000, she heard my message. She had been out of work for six months after being laid off from a high-paying "tech" job. She had house payments to make on her newly constructed home, which she had moved into two months before being laid off. But she continued to tithe to the Lord on her unemployment checks, and on her back vacation pay. She knew the Lord would provide.

When she heard my challenge to pledge the $2,000, she didn't have much to give. But that's when God gets the most glory!

Doria trusted God and pledged the entire $2,000, which she intended to pay on with her federal income tax return. In addition to this, she pledged to support the ministry monthly.

The following month, in May, her back vacation pay ran out. Now she was dependent on her unemployment checks, which were only about a quarter of her former income. But God saw her through these rough times. June came, and still nothing happened.

Then, in early July (exactly 90 days after she pledged the money) she was contacted by a recruiter who told her a Fortune 500 company wanted to hire her. God had provided!

Her new job paid $90,000 a year. She also received a sign-on bonus of $2,500 (God provided for the faith promise) and a relocation check for $10,000. To top it all off, this new job had an even better benefit package than the company for which she had previously worked.

She was faithful to God, and God was faithful to her. She ended up with more than she started with!

Listen, dear friend. I have seen God do extraordinary things when His people respond to Him in faith. Yet, I've also had situations in which people responded to a challenge God has given, and they did not receive the results they desired.

Perhaps there is a secret there—we must not give with our primary focus on being what God will do for us. We give, partnering with His purposes, generously contributing toward His mission.

God is excited when His children have generous spirits and trust Him. He never leaves His children in lack.

> Now to Him who is able to do exceedingly abundantly above all that we ask or think, according to the power that works in us, to Him be glory in the church by Christ Jesus to all generations, forever and ever. Amen (Ephesians 3:20-21).

CHAPTER 51

The $78,000 Miracle

When I was in Lexington, Kentucky, I met some other folks who took me up on that same challenge. It was a husband and wife—Curtis and Mary Lou.

Both of them had grown up in a religious church, but they had not heard much faith teaching.

Well, the Lord started to lead them in new ways. As they started watching Christian television programming, God began building their faith.

They saw this old preacher proclaiming God's word, demonstrating the Gospel of Christ. They told me later that I was instrumental in building their faith.

Now, like I've been telling you, I believe in planting seeds and expecting to reap a harvest. That's how God's financial system works. Curtis and Mary Lou learned about this as they watched their television. But as they watched, something I said scared them to death.

"Listen to what the man of God says. I want you to sow a $2,000 seed."

The reason this scared them was that they had made some bad financial decisions. They hadn't been walking in all the things that they believed. Also, they just were not familiar with the concept of sowing financial seeds and reaping a harvest.

This was a wake-up call for them. Yet, they didn't have the funds to make that kind of a pledge.

Now, when I challenge people like this, I know they don't have it. I'm trying to teach them how to trust in God.

This couple heard me talking about the pledge to be debt-free by sowing a seed, and even though they didn't have it, they took the challenge. They made a vow to God that they would send in any money that was above what they normally made. Then they made out a list of all the debt that they owed, believing for God to cancel them.

Over the next 90 days, the devil was after them. He didn't want them to get blessed, so he tried to choke off any extra money they received.

They were renting a building to a lady who decided to move out during the first month after their pledge. That was November.

They had also been receiving rent money from a man that was staying with them. In December, the second month after their pledge, he moved out. That cost them more money.

In January, to top it all off, the transmission in their car went out!

They were really being tested! But they were determined to trust God and honor their promise to Him. They weren't going to let the devil defeat them.

By the end of the 90 days, they had managed to pay the entire $2,000 pledge off. And then came the best part.

At the time, Mary Lou had an appeal with the government. It had been pending since 1992. The government owed them some money. It was their faith that triggered the blessing.

In a short time, that appeal went through, and they received a check in the mail for $63,000—from the U.S. government! Now that is a miracle!

As if that wasn't enough, there is even more to their story.

When Mary Lou found out that I was bringing my tent to Lexington in 2001, she made another pledge. That area had never received this kind of ministry before, and she wanted to help bring it to pass. So she pledged to send me $1,000. She didn't have that sum, but she sent what she had—only $10—trusting that God would provide the rest.

Well, just a few days before my crusade started, she received another letter in the mail from the government. They said that they had made a mistake, and that they actually owed her and her husband more money—over $15,000 more!

Hallelujah! God provided the rest of the pledge and more. Oh, this just blesses me to see this outstanding miracle. When my tent crusade started there in Lexington, this precious couple came up to the platform to testify. You should have heard the shouting that went on in that tent when they told their story!

I get so thrilled when God honors the faith of His children, especially those who are just learning. Although they were a little frightened, they moved in faith, and God honored that faith.

Sometimes God will ask you to give something that seems impossible to give. Don't hold back. When He speaks, you can trust His promises.

CHAPTER 52

The Angel and the Real Estate

One of the greatest testimonies, I believe, that I have heard regarding the $2,000 challenge was given by a dear elderly woman in one of my meetings. She put God to the test, and He proved faithful.

This woman was watching my telecast and heard me talking about the faith promise. She sat there and thought to herself, *I'm going to put God to the test.*

That's what I tell people to do. Put Him to the test!

So she wrote a check out for $200, the tithe on the pledge. She addressed it, put a stamp on it, and laid it on the coffee table. The next morning, she took it to the post office.

When she returned home, before she could set her purse down, there was a knock at the door. She didn't see anybody pull in behind her. Nobody had followed her in. But suddenly there was this knock at the door.

She opened the door, and there was a man standing there. "I want to buy some land," he said.

Now, this dear lady owned eight acres of land. She had tried to sell it. She went to nearly every realtor in town. They all told her it wouldn't sell because there were three high-powered gas lines through it. They told her the land couldn't be used for anything.

She told the visitor, "I've got some. But I don't guess you'll want it." She told him the truth about the land—why she couldn't sell it—but he wanted to see it anyway.

So she took him out there to see it. To her amazement, he said, "I'll tell you what. I'll give you $100,000 for it."

Wow! What a miracle! On the very same day, God provided because she was obedient to what the man of God told her to do.

You see, that's what I mean. When you hear the man or woman of God say something you wonder, "Are they just talking?" But when you step out in faith, you're not just being obedient to what a person says, you are being obedient to what God Himself says, speaking through the channel of a preacher.

When she testified under the tent, she told me that the weeds have grown on that property, and nobody has seen that man since. I believe it was an angel of the Lord!

Chapter 53

Cow Money

Years ago in Seattle, two tornadoes tore through and destroyed our tent. Now, it was the devil that caused this disaster. But God can take a disaster, turn it around, and work it for His glory.

We could not continue services in the tent, so I looked for a building. The Civic Auditorium was available over the next 17 days. We didn't miss a meeting. And before we left town, enough money came in to buy a brand-new tent.

The devil just doesn't have any sense. The old tent that he destroyed was full of holes anyway. Now we had a brand-new one!

But it was a 12-year-old boy that started the whole thing off.

I received the offering one night, and I happened to see a little boy walking down the aisle with a $5 bill in his hand. Tears were running down his face. You know how we human beings often make snap judgments and form first impressions? I thought, *I wonder what that kid is crying for? His mama gave him that five dollars. Maybe he just didn't want to walk down with her with it.*

He headed right for the bucket that I was holding. I said, "What are you crying for, boy?"

He threw the five dollars in the bucket and said, "Brother Schambach, that's my cow in there!"

I looked in the bucket and said, "Your what?"

I knew I had a story there, so I put the bucket in on of the pastor's hands. I took the little boy aside and said, "Tell me about it."

"I always wanted a cow of my own," he said. "But we lived in the city limits, and there's an ordinance that says you can't have cow in the backyard. But nine months ago, Dad moved out into the country. He called me and said I could have a cow now—but I had to pay for it. For nine months I've been saving my dimes. I've been running errands. I picked up a paper route. I get up at four in the morning and deliver newspapers. I've been saving five dollars for nine months."

I said, "Why are you putting that cow money in?"

He said, "I heard God's voice."

My God, that's the miracle to me! Giving five dollars is no miracle. But to see a 12-year-old boy obey the voice of the Lord that way! I asked him, "How did you know it was God?"

He said, "He called me by name. He said if I gave the cow money, He would give me the cow."

I looked at him and said, "Are you sure God told you that?"

"Yes, sir. He told me that."

I said, "Then dry up those tears! You're getting the best end of the deal!"

While the other folks were bringing their offerings, I sort of held onto his shoulder. I told all those people in that Civic Auditorium what I just told you about that boy.

Then a big six-feet-seven, 270-pound man in bib overalls got up. He started crying. He walked up, and I said, "What are you crying for, brother?"

He said, "God just spoke to me."

I said, "What did God tell you?"

He said, "He told me to give that boy a cow."

I looked up and down at him. I learned this lesson a long time ago: the folks with the fancy suits don't have the money. It's the guys wearing the overalls. The guys with the suits on have all their money in the suits!

So I kind of did a double take on him and said, "Brother, do you have a cow?"

"I've got thousands of them, Brother Schambach," he replied. He was the biggest rancher in the state of Washington. When God told that boy to give, He already had a cow waiting!

The following Saturday this rancher had a Polaroid picture shot of the boy with his cow. He said to me, "Brother Schambach, I wish you could have been out at the ranch today. That boy came out with his daddy in a rented trailer to pick up his cow. I told him to go pick out any one he wanted. You know, that rascal picked the best one I had! And he never even thanked me for it. He just put his arm around that cow and raised the other arm up and said, 'Thank you, Jesus, for my cow!'"

He knew exactly Who to thank—the cattle on a thousand hills belongs to God! (See Psalm 50:10.) God surely knows how to speak to a rancher to turn one of them loose.

After that little boy told his story, you should have seen how much money came in that offering. You don't have to beg people to give. You show them how God blesses and they'll want to get in on that blessing.

God was teaching that boy a principle, and teaching me a principle through that boy.

CHAPTER 54

Tithing Eggs

When I was in Bible school, my wife and I would go out into the hills of Missouri every Sunday morning, and I would preach in a one-room schoolhouse. Farmers from all over that area would come. One little precious lady, 83 years of age, would walk three miles, take her stockings off, and wade through a creek just to come and hear me preach. Even *I* wouldn't do that to hear *me* preach! (I was still learning how!)

She invited us to her home for dinner. She told us to park the car when we got to the creek and walk the rest of the way. We took our shoes off and waded through the creek, just like she did every Sunday. But that Sunday morning I was preaching on a difficult doctrinal subject—tithing. I said, "Ten cents out of every dollar you ever get a hold of belongs to God."

There they sat with smiles on their faces—which I knew was the wrong reaction. I wasn't getting the message through to them. So I said it again, and still they smiled. Finally it dawned on me, *You know why they're smiling? They don't have any money, and 10 percent of nothing is nothing! So I have to come at it from another way.*

It's amazing what comes out of you when you're anointed. I said, "If you have ten cows, one of those cows belongs to God." All the smiles left.

I knew they understood it now.

I said, "If you have 200 acres, 20 of them belong to God."

Nobody was smiling now.

After the service, a redheaded farmer came up to me, hands in his overall pockets. He said, "If my chickens lay 100 eggs every day, does God get 10 of the eggs?"

I said, "You got the message, brother. It's gratifying to know you got the message."

Without batting an eyelash, he looked me right in the eye and said, "You're not getting my eggs! The chickens aren't laying anyway!"

I said, "You know why those chickens aren't laying? Because you're robbing God! Those chickens can't even live a normal life!"

I didn't know how right I was. Remember, I was just learning. He looked at me and said, "You mean to tell me if I give God what belongs to Him, those chickens will lay more eggs? Wait here!"

He got into that pickup truck and went back to the farm and brought a brown sack full of eggs. He laid them down at the altar. He came back to me, hands in his overalls, and said, "You going to be here next Sunday?"

I said, "Yes, sir."

He said, "This better work!"

I was so young in the Lord, I didn't know whether it was going to work or not. I went back to the Bible that week. I didn't get much studying done. But I got a whole lot of praying done. I was praying, "Lord, bless those chickens! Lord, give them a double portion! Let them lay double yolks, Lord!"

The next Sunday, my wife and I headed out to that little town. I said, "Honey, do you see anybody standing in that schoolhouse?"

She said, "I believe somebody's there."

I said, "Does it have red hair?"

She said, "I'm not close enough to see that, yet."

Sure enough, it was Red waiting for me. But I couldn't see his face. I didn't know whether he was mad or glad. I brought my old DeSoto to a halt and pulled on the emergency brake. Old Red came running to the car. I don't ever like to be at a disadvantage, so I jumped out of the car. He grabbed hold of me and started dancing me around that DeSoto.

"Preach, man, it worked, brother!" he cried. "Praise God, it worked! It worked!"

I breathed easy for the first time all week. Then I looked around and said, "Hold it, Red, wait! Where's the tithe?" I believed I had a right to ask him for that. I said, "If we made the thing work, where's the tithe?"

Hands still in his overalls, he said, "In there, at the altar, Preach. Brought 'em early today."

I walked into that one-room schoolhouse, and sitting in front of that altar was a whole crate of eggs—25 dozen. I looked at him and said, "What did you do, bring them *all*?"

His hands were still in his overalls. "Just the tithe, Preach. Just the tithe." From a brown sack to 25 dozen!

He threw his arms around me and said, "Preacher, I ain't going to rob God no more."

I looked at him and said, "Me neither."

I believe we've all had an apple out of that bag. Then we wonder why we're not blessed.

God rewards obedience.

CHAPTER 55

Don't Eat Your Seed

I want to talk to you pastors out there. Listen to me, God wants to bless you, too!

I have seen God pull churches out of debt. I've seen it here in America, in Europe, in Canada—all over the world. Everywhere I go I preach about the blessing that comes from giving to God.

I want all of you that are in the ministry to pay close attention to this story.

There was a woman named Sharon who was pastoring a church with her husband in Bellis, Alberta, Canada. One night they were watching television and saw me preach a sermon on the miracle of giving.

They were in a desperate situation. If they didn't have $40,000 very soon, their church was going to be shut down. But when they heard the message, faith came alive in their hearts.

They phoned the television station and pledged to give to God. Now, they didn't have the money, but they believed that God would provide.

Two days later, they received $1,000 from an unexpected source.

Now, they needed this money desperately. But they had made a promise to give to the Lord, to plant a seed.

Listen, folks, you can't eat your seed! Don't worry, God can provide $40,000 just as easily as he can provide $1,000. If you do what He tells you to do, He will take care of you.

So even though they needed that $1,000, they sent it in.

Fourteen days later, a $40,000 check was put in their hands!

Hear me, pastors. It works! They were at the bottom. They didn't have anything. But they stood on God's Word and planted a seed, and then they reaped a great harvest.

Is your church in financial trouble? Then exercise your faith and plant a seed. I'm telling you, when you give to God, He's going to meet the need. You cannot out-give God!

CHAPTER 56

Multiplying Money

I had a tent up over in East St. Louis some years ago. I'll never forget a little woman—she must have been 68 years of age—who came to me. (I believe she must have gone to be with the Lord by now.) She said to me, "Brother Schambach, I want you to pray that God will let me rent a bus."

I thought, *What in the world would she want a bus for? That's the craziest request I have ever heard.* So I asked her why she wanted a bus. She said, "I want to take a crowd of people to hear Kathryn Kuhlman."

I said, "You want me to pray and ask God to give you money to get a bus so you can take a crowd of people out of my tent meeting to go hear a woman preach?" But I prayed. I asked God to bless her with it.

She said, "I already have $400, but I need a little over $800."

I took the paper sack of money she had, and I prayed. On Monday night she came back shouting. I never saw a woman that old shout like she did. She said, "Brother Schambach, I went home and counted that money; there was $500. I called my husband to count it; I thought I made a mistake. He sat down and counted it, and he got $600. I put it back into the bag, took it down to the bank the next morning and had the bankers count it. They counted $700." The teller asked if she wanted to deposit it, but she didn't. She had the money put back into the bag. She took that bag down to the Greyhound Bus rental and said, "Here's my money for the bus." When they counted, there was a little over $800—enough to get her bus. She took a busload of people to hear Kathryn Kuhlman preach.

The Lord will provide! He will satisfy the hunger pains of the people. He rented a bus for a woman. I don't care what your need is; Jesus is a miracle-working God, and He will perform a miracle in your life!

What is your need? You know, people get into a rut many times, and they consider miracles only in the aspect of healing. But God is a miracle-working God in *every phase of life!*

Chapter 57

No Sense, Just Faith

I'll never forget the first church building I bought. It was an Old Jewish YWHA in New Jersey. I rented it for three months, preached in it, and so many folks got saved in it, I thought I might as well just buy the building and establish a church. But there was no way to do it—I didn't even have a bank account.

One day, while we were still renting, I was studying my message. I was going to preach on Deuteronomy 11:24, which says, "Every place on which the sole of your foot treads shall be yours…." Oh, Lord! I knew I wasn't just preaching to those people, I was preaching to myself.

I laid hands on about 500 people that night, but I couldn't wait to close that service. After it was over, I got my Bible, went out, and I said to some of my preacher friends, "Come with me. We're going to walk around the building and lay some footprints down. I'm going to claim this thing."

I couldn't buy it. I had never had a bank account. I had never written a check. I didn't have any sense, but I had faith.

When I told my preacher friends that I was going to walk around that building and claim it, they said, "We'll wait in the car. You go ahead and walk."

I've learned this: When you put your faith to work, sometimes you have to do it all by yourself. God said every bit of ground that the soles of your feet tread on, you shall possess it.

I walked around that building, and the next day they put a "For Sale" sign on the lawn. I pulled it out, marched down to the realtor's office, and asked him, "Who put this on my property?" He thought I was crazy, since he knew I had been renting the place.

He said, "What do you want to offer me for that building?"

I said, "Nothing."

"Well," he said, "come back when you have money."

I said, "Now hold on here a minute. I believe in starting low."

He said, "We just had an offer of $265,000. An insurance company owns it, and I know they won't sell for less than that."

Just then the Holy Ghost said, "Offer them $75,000." Now, if He had told me to offer $1 million, I would have done it, because I didn't have a dime anyway. There's no difference between $75,000 and $1 million if you don't have anything at all. Zero is zero. That's why it's always good to obey God. You don't have to be afraid of anything. You started with nothing; you're going to end with nothing.

I said, "I'll give you $75,000."

He didn't want to do it, but when I insisted, he picked up the phone and called the chairman of the board of this insurance company. Turning away from me, I could hear him say, "I have a crazy preacher in my office. I told him you folks turned down an offer of $265,000, but he told me to offer you $75,000. I told him there's no way you'll do it. And…what did you say? Would you say that one more time? Well, all right. It's your building. Yes, sir."

He hung up the phone and turned around to me. "He told me to sell it to you for $75,000."

I said, "What happened?"

Dumbfounded, that realtor explained, "The board of directors were meeting when I called. They had such a great year in life insurance that they said to give it to the preacher for $75,000, and they would take a loss on the taxes. You're not so dumb after all, are you, preacher?"

I said, "No, sir."

He said, "Now, how much money do you have for a down payment?"

I said, "Nothing."

He asked for $35,000 down. God provided $25,000. But the night before I had to come up with the money, we were still $10,000 short, and I didn't know what we'd do. A local preacher asked me, "What are you going to do?"

I said, "Nothing. I didn't do anything when I first started; I'm not going to do anything now. There's no time to worry now. There's no way God's going to let the devil whip Him in a business deal. God's the best businessman I've ever seen. He always finishes what He starts."

I sat in that office the next day and waited until ten minutes before noon. Noon was the deadline! Then a little woman came walking up. I ran out to her and said, "Give it to me! Give it to me!"

She said, "How do you know I have something for you?"

I said, "I'll talk to you later; just turn it loose and give it to me. It's got to be you. God's never cut it so close!" She reached into her purse and took out a $10,000 cashier's check. I grabbed that thing and went down to the bank. The building belonged to me!

After it was over, one of those preachers who wouldn't march around the building with me in the first place called me on the phone from Englewood and said, "I found a building here in Englewood that I want for a church. Come on over and walk around it for me."

I said, "Well, I'm about 28 minutes from you, but I'll make it in 20. Wait for me. But remember, brother, if I use my feet, it's going to be my building!"

He never even bothered to hang up—just left the phone dangling and ran over to that building. He didn't just march around it; he raced around it and laid down his size ten tracks. And guess what? God gave him his building!

God has a specific inheritance for you! Learn how to trust Him, and He'll lead you right to it!

I didn't have a lick of sense. I just had faith. And God brought me through. I do have one regret, though—I wish I would have walked around the whole block!

Chapter 58

Conclusion
"The Miracle of Giving"

Give, and it will be given to you: good measure, pressed down, shaken together, and running over will be put into your bosom. For with the same measure that you use, it will be measured back to you (Luke 6:38).

Throughout the years I have learned an important truth—giving is a powerful tool for the miraculous.

God loves giving. It moves His heart. When we give, it is an expression of our total trust and obedience to God. Doors are opened in the supernatural realm when we give to God.

God wants to bless His people. He loves to pour out showers of blessing on those who serve Him. The testimonies that you are about to read will attest to that fact. Through these people's stories, you will see what the Lord can do through people who give to Him.

But listen to me. If we want the blessing of God in our lives, we must learn this principle: the blessing follows obedience.

"Will a man rob God? Yet you have robbed Me! But you say, 'In what way have we robbed You?' In tithes and offerings. You

237

are cursed with a curse, for you have robbed Me, even this whole nation. Bring all the tithes into the storehouse, that there may be food in My house, and try Me now in this," says the Lord of hosts, "If I will not open for you the windows of heaven and pour out for you such blessing that there will not be room enough to receive it" (Malachi 3:8-10).

Just imagine that. God wants to pour out a blessing on His people that's too big for them to receive!

But blessing only comes when we commit ourselves to obeying God by giving to Him. You cannot disobey God in the area of tithing without locking God's blessing out of your life. If you are a Christian, you should be going to the house of God weekly to worship, and you should pay your tithes there.

Too many individuals "worship" all week at the shopping mall shrines and pay more than tithes there. Then, when they come to the house of God they have nothing left to give. No wonder God's people are bound up with debt and financial difficulty.

You might say, "Brother Schambach, I would love to give to God, but I just don't have anything to give. I don't have any money."

Good! Since you don't have anything, you won't be able to take credit for it when God performs a miracle. He will get all the glory! God usually sends me to people who don't have anything. I have seen countless times how God has provided when there was a need, all because somebody stepped out in faith and planted a seed.

Listen, it's a biblical principle that when you step out in faith and plant, God will see to it that you reap a blessing.

God always has a miracle waiting for us if we'll just step out in faith and do what He's calling us to do. He will bless us beyond measure, not just financially, but in every other way, too. But He wants us to trust Him.

Now, anybody can trust Him when the checkbook is filled. But it takes faith to trust Him when the balance says "double zero." There's one thing that I've learned about God, though—He will make a way where there is no way.

If you are struggling in your finances, God wants to set you free. You do not have to be in bondage to debt or want. God wants you blessed. But you've got to step out on the water! You've got to let Him know that you mean business.

But this I say: He who sows sparingly will also reap sparingly, and he who sows bountifully will also reap bountifully. So let each one give as he purposes in his heart, not grudgingly or of necessity; for God loves a cheerful giver. And God is able to make all grace about toward you, that you, always having all sufficiency in all things, may have an abundance for every good work (2 Corinthians 9:6-8).

When you allow giving to be a way of life for you, it becomes a miracle tool in your hand.

Allow God to develop a giving heart in you. It may be hard at first, but God can help you to be a cheerful giver. Remember, you are not giving to man, who can sometimes be unthankful or careless. You are giving to God.

But now I want to pray for you. If you're struggling financially, agree with me now, and believe God to perform a miracle.

Father, I come to You in the name of Jesus. I bring these before You whose backs are against the wall. I come against the bondage of debt in their lives. Satan, you have got no business in their pocketbooks, so I command you right now to loose your hold on their finances. Lord, I pray that You develop in these individual giving hearts. And Lord, as they learn to give to You, I pray that You would open up the windows of heaven and pour out a blessing on them. Let it be above what they could even ask or think. Give them a testimony that will bring glory to You alone. In Jesus' name I pray. Amen and amen.

PART V

Miracles on FOREIGN SOIL

"All The World"

And He said to them, "Go into all the world and preach the gospel to every creature" (Mark 16:15).

I want you to know that we preach this message around the world—the saving, healing power of Christ. I have been to India, Russia, Bulgaria, Mexico, Brazil, Haiti, Indonesia—and many, many other places with this gospel of power. The Bible I preach has to work in Haiti—or India or Mozambique or Japan—just like it works here. If it doesn't work everywhere, then it's not the Bible. If it doesn't work everywhere, then it's not true. It has to work in other countries just like it works here in the United States. And let me tell you, it does! We see more miracles in foreign countries than we do here in the United States.

I remember going to Mexico City with T.L. Osborn, preaching to 60,000 people. I'll never forget praying just one prayer. Instantly, blind eyes were opened. Deaf ears came unstopped. No human hands were ever laid on them! Just one prayer! People were picking up their wheelchairs, holding them over their head, and wading up to the platform to give God praise!

If God can make it work in Atlanta, God can make it work in Haiti! God can make it work over in Sudan! I don't care where it is, God's Word is real—and it works!

Let me tell you, what God has done in other countries through this ministry will absolutely blow your mind!

CHAPTER 59

India

When I pastored a church in the early 1950s, we sponsored a missionary in India by paying his salary. He spent 30 years there—30 long years.

On one occasion, he told me something that discouraged me from even supporting him. He said he had spent 30 years in India and had never seen one Mohammedan born again. I said, "What kind of investment am I making? We are investing money and keeping that man in India to preach the Gospel and not one soul has been saved. It is time to rearrange our priorities." So I went to India to find out what was going on.

The first time I visited in 1956, I preached to 50,000 people. I visited all the market places. I saw beggars, blind folks, and people who couldn't walk. I have never seen so many sick people. India is one of the poorest nations in the world with so many homeless, penniless people.

We invested thousands of dollars to build a structure that protected people from the hot sun so that they could hear the Gospel.

On that opening day, I was so thrilled. I preached for two hours, and my interpreter translated for two hours—for a total of four hours. They wanted me to go on. When I gave the altar call, I was so disappointed. I had preached to 50,000 people, and not one soul had come to accept Jesus.

My mind went back to the missionary and I said, "Oh, Lord." But I knew God called us to do more than just preach the Word. He called us to demonstrate the Gospel.

Although no one came forward to accept Christ, and the crowd was obviously ready for the benediction, I said, "I am not done now. God says that signs follow His Word. I did what God called me to do; now I am going to let God do what He said He was going to do."

I invited three people from the audience to come forward—they were beggars. I knew who they were. One was blind, one was deaf and dumb, and the other was a crippled woman who had never walked upright. She walked in a horizontal position on the heels of her feet and the heels of her hands. She had a disease that hindered her from standing upright.

Fifty thousand people were watching. I laid hands on the blind woman first. I said, "In the name of Jesus, I command these blind eyes to see." Instantly, God opened her eyes and she ran through the audience, shouting in her own tongue, "I can see! I can see!"

I went to the deaf mute and put my fingers in his ears and my thumb on his tongue. I said, "In the name of Jesus, I command this deaf and dumb spirit to come out!" Instantly, the spirit responded and the man started speaking English within a few minutes. He didn't know his own language. He had been a deaf mute, but God had opened his ears and loosened his tongue.

It came time to pray for the crippled woman. I said, "Now I am going to lay hands on this woman in the name of Mohammed. I am going to give him equal time." My interpreter did not want to translate this statement. I said, "You do what I tell you to do, Mister. You are my interpreter. I am the man of God."

Not one person in the audience expected her to get up, because they knew Mohammed was dead. I said, "Now, that is the difference between the god you serve and the God I serve. I didn't come here to put your god down; I came to lift mine up. You visit your shrine. I visit mine, but mine is empty because He is no longer there. That is the difference between the tombs. I came to let you know my Jesus is not dead—He is alive, and He is the same today as He was yesterday."

I laid hands on the woman in the name of Mohammed and said, "Rise and walk in the name of Mohammed." Someone asked me what I would have done if she had gotten up. I guess I would have converted.

But she didn't get up. So I said, "I am going to use the name that is above every name, the name of Jesus—the Lamb that was slain for the world. Jesus died for the people of India and for the whole world." The woman had never taken an upright step in 58 years. I laid hands on her in the name of Jesus of Nazareth and said, "In the name of Jesus, rise and walk." She stood upright and walked for the first time in her life, because Jesus Christ is God!

Do you know what happened? The people in that crowd started jumping out of trees, and a mob came running toward me. I jumped behind my interpreter. I thought they were going to tar and feather me and run me out of their country. I never saw such an onslaught of people. They were yelling something at the top of their voices. I asked my interpreter, "What are they saying?"

He said, "They are hollering, 'Jesus is alive! Jesus is the Christ! Jesus is God!' They are coming to get saved." What a thrill! Not one of them came when I preached, but when they saw the demonstration of the Gospel, they came.

God has called the Church to demonstrate His power. Aren't you glad He is alive today?

> *Then Philip went down to the city of Samaria and preached Christ to them. And the multitudes with one accord heeded the things spoken by Philip, hearing and seeing the miracles which he did (Acts 8:5-6).*

Chapter 60

Haiti

Haiti is one of the poorest nations in our hemisphere. The first time I flew to Haiti, I was met by a group of preachers. Instead of greeting me with "Welcome to Haiti," they looked at me and said, "You're not taking an offering here!"

I said, "When is the next plane out of here? You men didn't call for me. The Holy Ghost sent me down here. I'm going to take an offering, because the Bible instructs us to teach our people to give."

"But our people have no money! We're pastors. We don't even receive an offering."

I said, "Then I hold you gentlemen responsible for the poverty of your nation. If I can't make this Bible work in Haiti, I'll burn the thing. Either it's the truth or it's a lie; either it's God's book or it's man's book. I believe it's God's book."

I began to preach to the people and receive an offering from them. Those poor people opened their hearts in a wonderful way and gave about $15,000. At that time, that was unheard of in the history of Haiti. I told those pastors, "Your people need to learn the Gospel here in Haiti like people know it in Atlanta and New York City! If people can make it work there, they can make it work here!"

I told them the story of a little widow woman who attended my church in inner-city Brooklyn, Mother Valez. She taught me this lesson. One service, she came to me and said, "God told me to give my rent money in the offering."

I asked her, "Mother, when is your rent due?"

"In three days," she said.

I didn't want to take her rent money. No way! I was her pastor, and I didn't want to see her in financial difficulty. I rolled that money back into her hand and told her to pay the rent.

I'll never forget what she said to me.

"Are you trying to cheat me out of my blessing? You didn't ask for it, God did! Now take it!"

She hit me where it hurt. So I took her offering, humbled by her response. That woman taught me something.

Later on that week Mother Valez came to church with another offering. Not only did God pay the rent, but she had even more to give back to Him.

That wasn't the best part of her testimony, though. She and I had been praying for her sons to be saved. She said, "Brother Schambach, those two boys you and I have been praying and fasting for got saved this morning!"

This story blesses me so much because it illustrates the point that God blesses those who give, even when they are facing financial difficulty. I told this story to the people in Haiti.

The next night a little Haitian woman came to me with $100. Seventy thousand people were there for that service, and I wanted all of them to hear what this little lady had to say.

She said, "Remember that story Pastor told last night about that woman in Brooklyn? If God can do it in Brooklyn, He can do it here in Haiti. My rent is $160, and it's due tomorrow. I only have $100. So I'm just going to give it to God. They won't take it anyway. I'm going to trust God to do it!"

I thought, *Oh, Lord.*

And all the Haitian preachers on the platform were sitting there saying, "Oh, Lord. This ain't New York. This is Port-au-Prince."

All of a sudden, I saw a man coming from the middle of that crowd. He said, "God spoke to me. He told me to pay that woman's rent for three months. Here's the check for it."

Another time in Haiti, I conducted a revival crusade in a stadium in Port-au-Prince, Haiti, one year. On opening night, there were 35,000 people in that stadium. That night, I prayed a prayer for the people and left.

While I was going out, this little 12-year-old boy wrapped his hands around my leg and would not turn loose. While I was dragging him, he was saying something in Creole. I couldn't understand him, so I asked, "What in the world is he saying?"

My driver said, "I'll interpret for you. This boy is telling you he was born blind. When you prayed that one prayer, the lights came on. He can see!"

I picked that boy up and put him in the arms of one of the preachers and said, "Take him up there and let him tell the story." When we were driving out, it sounded like somebody had made a touchdown in there! The people had heard the boy's testimony.

Now, everybody in Port-au-Prince knew that boy. He had begged on the streets, and everyone knew he was totally blind. The news of his miracle spread, and the next night you couldn't get near the stadium. It was jam-packed with about 70,000 people, and many more outside who couldn't get in.

That triggered many more miracles throughout the entire crusade.

CHAPTER 61

Trinidad

I conducted crusades in Trinidad, down in the Caribbean, among the poor folks down there. I followed Dan Betzer, the radio speaker for the Assemblies of God organization. He was there a week before me. I came in to close it out. I was there for three nights. The missionary who put this event on said, "Brother Schambach, the budget for this entire revival is $38,000." I think he was trying to tell me something, but I didn't care what the budget was. I was a guest. He asked me to come down and preach.

So I said, "Well, you've been going on here about three weeks. You probably have it already met. How much has come in so far?"

He said, "Four thousand dollars."

I said, "You had better let me take the offering tonight."

Trinidad is 50 percent black and 50 percent Indian. There are a lot of Indians from India; they have immigrated there. It was a mixed audience that night. God started performing miracles. Blind eyes began to open. Demons were cast out. When God begins to manifest His power, the first thing people want to do is give God something. I prayed and asked God to touch the hearts of the people to give. That night, when I received the offering, $70,000 came in.

The missionary cried all night long. He couldn't sleep. The next night we went back. I said, "We don't have to receive offerings now; the meeting is paid for."

But people came and said, "I didn't have it last night. I want to give tonight." And it was more than the previous night. In three nights' time, $210,000—in Trinidad! Of course, we left it all there for the churches. I didn't even spend a dime of it. One gentleman brought me five $100 bills and said, "I just want you to take these home as a souvenir."

I said, "Nothing doing. That's going in the offering. I'm not taking anything out of here. We came to give it to God."

Now I told this same story to a full-gospel businessmen's meeting. I said, "If I can raise an offering of $70,000 down in Trinidad, I had better do more than that tonight." In five minutes, $200,000 came in— enough to pay every bill they had. God is a miraculous God!

CHAPTER 62

The Caribbean

By now you should know that I am so thankful for the means of radio to preach the Gospel. It has been a tried and true method of reaching people all across this nation. Well, it's not different anywhere else. Thousands of people in foreign nations have been blessed by our broadcasts all over the world.

In the 1970s, my old church, Philadelphia Miracle Temple, was sponsoring my radio broadcasts in the Caribbean. I knew these people needed the Gospel, too. Yet, I wasn't sure if we were really reaching them.

So I decided to conduct a long crusade throughout the Caribbean. I wanted to see of the investment Philadelphia Miracle Temple was making was really touching lives. This crusade went from the Virgin Islands to St. Kitts, St. Vincent, Trinidad, and the Port of Spain.

In St. Kitts, 35,000 people showed up for the first meeting—on an island with a population of just 50,000!

When I met the governor of St. Kitts, he told me, "The entire island comes to a halt when your radio broadcast airs each day." Wow!

There was a mighty demonstration of the power of God. During that meeting, 50 people jumped out of wheelchairs! And so many deaf ears were unstopped that the school for the deaf there in St. Kitts had to be shut down! Hallelujah!

Now, that crusade service was broadcast on live radio to the island of Antigua. It shook them up, too!

The next day a delegation from Antigua came and begged me to preach on their island. Of course, I hadn't planned to go there. My schedule was full as it was, and I only had two days of rest planned during the entire crusade. Now, I'm human. I get tired just like everybody else. I told them this, but they just wouldn't take no for an answer.

"You can rest after the rapture!" they said. "We need you in Antigua now."

So I went, and God moved miraculously.

I never had to wonder again whether the Caribbean broadcasts were reaching people!

CHAPTER 63

Indonesia

I want to share with you some amazing stories that took place in Indonesia. But first, I want to say a little bit about the baptism of the Holy Ghost.

I'm not ashamed to preach about the baptism of the Holy Ghost. A lot of preachers don't believe in this, or they are ashamed to speak it from the pulpit. Not me! I like to shout it from the rooftops. I like to splash it all over TV and radio. I like to let people know that God wants to fill them with the Holy Ghost and fire!

Read with me in Acts 2:1-4:

When the Day of Pentecost had fully come, they were all with one accord in one place. And suddenly there came a sound from heaven, as of a rushing mighty wind, and it filled the whole house where they were sitting. Then there appeared to them divided tongues, as of fire, and one sat upon each of them. And they were all filled with the Holy Spirit and began to speak with other tongues, as the Spirit gave them utterance.

The record is very clear that the tongues of fire sat upon each of them, and they were all filled with the Holy Ghost. And when they were all filled with the Holy Ghost, they began to speak in tongues as the Spirit gave them utterance. Before the day of Pentecost, there is no record that any person ever spoke an unlearned language as a result of the moving of God's Spirit.

In Acts 2, it talks of a "rushing mighty wind," "tongues, as of fire," and says that they were speaking "with other tongues." Later in Acts 10, it says they were speaking with tongues and magnifying God. Finally, in Acts 19, it refers to speaking with tongues and prophecy.

In each instance, there was an additional manifestation, but only speaking with tongues occurred every time. You see, this was to be the initial evidence that believers had been filled with the Holy Ghost. It signified that the early church had received "the promise of the Father" and "the Comforter" that Jesus had promised.

Well, the Holy Ghost is just as real to us in this day as He was for the early church. I have experienced this many times, but one of the greatest examples I have seen came when I was preaching in Indonesia. Thirty thousand people gathered on a field to hear me preach.

Now, I was tired. I had been preaching all through that area. I had preached to so many people, and I was really tired in my body. When I was getting ready to preach that day, I prayed, "Oh, Lord. Please spare this old flesh of mine. Let Your Spirit come on everybody that's out in that field."

All of a sudden, 10,000 people fell out under the power of God. Like a breath of wind! I looked in front of me, and 10,000 more people fell out. Then I looked to the side, and the last 10,000 people fell out. Right there in front of me! No catchers. They were all fallers, and they all fell out right on the field.

There I was, standing all by myself. So I looked around at my interpreter, and he was out! I said, "Lord, I feel like I've been left out. Knock me out, too."

God said, "Walk through the crowd of the people."

So I walked out there. Toward the back, there was group of young people, Indonesian young people. They were speaking in English. In English! It blew my mind.

I ran up and got my interpreter off the ground. I said, "Get up quick!"

"What?" he replied. "What do you want me to do?"

I said, "Come with me. I want you to see and hear what I found."

So he came back with me and I showed him.

"You got me up out of the Spirit for this?" he said. "Oh, Brother Schambach, that's a common occurrence. They're receiving the Holy Ghost. They don't know English, but this is a sign to them that they received the baptism of the Holy Ghost."

You see, I know English. It's not an unknown tongue to me. It wasn't to my interpreter either. He knew English as well as his native language. But these young people didn't know English. Nobody had ever taught them this. It was the utterance of the Holy Spirit. That was the initial evidence to them.

You might be wondering about the baptism of the Holy Ghost. Your pastor might tell you that it's not for today, or that it's not for everyone today, just some. Well, I'm telling you it's for you.

God has provided a mighty in-filling of the Holy Ghost and power to carry His people over the turbulent times of these last days. You need this! It is for you! Let God baptize you in the Holy Ghost and fire!

There was another miracle that took place in Indonesia that blew my mind. I cannot explain how it happened. All I know is that it happened.

I was conducting meetings in Semarang. On the opening night, there was torrential downpour. I mean, everything was drenched. (I really know when to have an outdoor meeting!) But the place was still packed. Not one of those people moved. They stood there and listened to me preach.

Some of my associates wanted to give me an umbrella to put over me, but I said, "No. If they're going to stand in the rain to hear me, I'm going to preach to them in the rain."

So I preached to them in the rain! And God did so many great miracles that day. I laid hands on people. Blind eyes were opened. Deaf ears were unstopped. Cripples were walking. It was powerful!

Because of the large crowd, there were army guards all around. They'd never had crowds of that capacity before. One of these soldiers, who was a colonel in the army and a Muslim, came to me and said, "Would you pray for me?"

"What's wrong with you?" I said.

"Well, I got shot in this eye. The bullet is still in there, and I can't see out of that eye."

Now, I knew this man was a Muslim. So I made it clear to him what name I pray in—the name of Jesus. He is the only miracle-worker. Mohammed can't hear me pray because he is still in the grave. But Jesus is alive! Hallelujah!

"I pray in the name of Jesus," I told him.

"Use any name you want," he replied. "I've seen too much here!"

So I prayed for that colonel in the name of Jesus. I can't explain what happened after that. It is hard to fathom! I am not a chemist. I'm not a scientist. But after I put my hand on that eye and asked God to perform a miracle, the bullet melted right into my hand, and God restored perfect vision to the eye.

That man got saved and filled with the Spirit, and God called him to preach.

Now, he would have been up for retirement in six months, but he went immediately and resigned his commission! He said, "I want to travel all over Indonesia and tell my people that Jesus is Lord!"

Listen to me. He wasn't saved when God performed the miracle. He was still a sinner. Many Christians don't like to hear that. But God did it anyway, and it was that miracle that opened his eyes to the Gospel, and to the power of Jesus Christ. Then God used him to shake up Indonesia!

There was another Muslim man who came to me for a miracle in Suribia, Indonesia. But this one was not a soldier. He was a priest.

He brought his wife to me, who was demon-possessed. Doctors couldn't help her. His religion couldn't help her. She was bound by the devil.

So he brought her to me for prayer. Then when I laid hands on her, the strangest thing happened. All of a sudden, there were thumbtacks and nails coming out of her skin. I've never seen anything like it before. God delivered her and set her free.

The next night the man came back to the service. While I was receiving the offering, he came up to the front and threw something in the bucket. It was wrapped up in a newspaper, and was so heavy that the bucket fell out of my hand.

I grabbed him by the shoulder and pulled him back. I said, "What in the world do you got in there?"

"Look," he said.

I opened it up and discovered that it was a brick of solid gold!

Then he told his story: "I've had my wife everywhere. Doctors couldn't do anything. My religion couldn't do anything. I brought her here and you laid hands on her in the name of Jesus, and she was delivered. I answered that altar call, and now I'm a Jesus man. And I wanted to bring you that offering."

I gave the gold to our missionary there and told him to build a new home for orphans.

CHAPTER 64

Africa

In Africa, in a church with a crowd of 6,000 people, I suddenly stopped preaching. In the back there was a man sitting in the aisle, talking with his hands. I knew he was interpreting for the deaf. The anointing of God came on me. I stopped and said, "Brother, you back there in that aisle, you are disturbing me." He wasn't saying anything vocally, but he was conveying my message to people who couldn't hear. I wanted to capture his attention. And you know I did when I said that. I continued, "Brother, I am getting tired of you talking while I am talking. Bring all those deaf folks up here. God is going to heal them now."

Seventeen of them got up—seventeen deaf mutes in Africa. I lined them up on the platform facing the people. Cameras were on. We were on television. The pastor of the church was nervously sitting on the edge of his chair.

I looked at the deaf people and saw one boy smiling from ear to ear.

"Yeah," I said to myself, "he's expecting something."

I had been preaching that Jesus Christ is the same today as He was yesterday. Well, if you believe that, demonstrate it. Paul said:

And I, brethren, when I came to you, did not come with excellence of speech or of wisdom declaring to you the testimony of God.... And my speech and my preaching were not with persuasive words of human wisdom, but in demonstration of the Spirit and of power, that your faith should not be in the wisdom of men but in the power of God (1 Corinthians 2:1,4-5).

I believe in what I preach. So I began to talk to that boy. I don't know sign language, so the man started to interpret. I said, "I don't need you anymore. Go sit down."

I put my finger in the boy's ears and in the name of Jesus took authority over that deaf and dumb spirit. I felt the spirit slide right by my finger. I knew he had come out—I knew it! I knew the boy's ears had opened. I spent about ten minutes with the lad and started teaching him English.

The pastor of the church was so blessed, he did a somersault in mid-air—and he was not an acrobat!

I went down the line. I got a hold of a woman, cast that spirit out of her, and taught her to speak. I said to the pastor, "Bring the rest of your pastors here." There were 35 of them. I said, "Line them up. I am not going to wear myself out. Let them wear themselves out. Tell them to put their fingers in the people's ears. Tell them to put a thumb on their tongues. I will pray one prayer, and God will heal all 15 of them."

I prayed one prayer, talked to that deaf and dumb spirit, and in the name of Jesus commanded it to come out. The pastor took the microphone on television and went down the line. Each one heard and spoke!

"What Do You Want?"

Then Jesus went out from there and departed to the region of Tyre and Sidon. And behold, a woman of Canaan came from that region and cried out to Him, saying, "Have mercy on me, O Lord, Son of David! My daughter is severely demon-possessed." But He answered her not a word. And His disciples came and urged Him, saying, "Send her away, for she cries out after us." But He answered and said, "I was not sent except to the lost sheep of the house of Israel." Then she came and worshipped Him, saying, "Lord, help me!" But He answered and said, "It is not good to take the children's bread and throw it to the little dogs." And she said, "Yes, Lord, yet even the little dogs eat the crumbs which fall from their masters' table." Then Jesus answered and said to her, "O woman, great is your faith! Let it be to you as you desire." And her daughter was healed from that very hour (Matthew 15:21-28).

This woman came to Jesus with a need. When she looked into His eyes, she saw a delivering power greater than any she had.

It seemed at first that Jesus was putting her off, but He was not. He was simply telling the truth.

His mission was to preach salvation to the Jews. According to His call and mission, there was no way He could give this woman a miracle. But her faith caused her to press in and receive a miracle anyway! She would not take no for an answer—even from Jesus. That's some kind of faith!

Friend, if you are a child of God, you don't have to beg like this woman did. You have been washed in the Blood of the Lamb. There is a table of God's goodness set out for you. All the power, anointing, gifts, and fruits of God's Spirit belong to you. Partake of them. Enjoy them. Let God know you appreciate what He has prepared for you. Hallelujah!

Jesus, in response to this woman's refusal to be denied, said something He never said to Peter, James, or John. He said, "O woman, great is your faith; Let it be to you as you desire." In today's language, that means, "Whatever you want, you've got it!"

And this brings up a point worth looking at: He didn't say, "What My will is, let that happen to you." He said, "Let it be to you as *you* desire."

Let me get really personal here for a moment, friend. What do you want from the Lord today? I hear people say, "Well, anything He wants to give me." But you see, that isn't the way faith works. He wants to know exactly what you want.

Perhaps you have loved ones who are facing great needs today. I want to encourage you again that you can stand in their place before Jesus and plead their cause. This is what intercession is all about.

Maybe it's you that has the need. I don't care whether it's for healing, deliverance, financial freedom—whatever it is, God wants to do it for you.

I trust that your faith has come alive as you have read these wonderful testimonies of God's miracle-working power. I'm here to tell you that what He did for these people, He'll do for you. You see, God is no respecter of persons. If He does something for one person, He will do it for everybody who will believe Him for it.

Psalm 34:19 says, *"Many are the afflictions of the righteous, but the Lord **delivers him out of them all**."* Not half of them. Not most of them. Not even 99.9 percent of them. The Bible says *all* of them!

You say, "Well, I've prayed and nothing happens." Well, keep on praying! Keep on asking! Don't give up. It's not over 'til it's over! You are coming out of this situation. You are going to be more than a conqueror. Hallelujah!

Press your way through. You don't know how close you are to your miracle! All you've got to do is keep on exercising your faith. God will do the rest. He has a miracle with your name written all over it!

Remember, the Bible says everyone who asks receives. That's you! That's me! That's everybody!

So get ready. Put your faith in God, and you will be in a position to receive the greatest miracle that you have ever experienced.

About the Author

R.W. Schambach is a bold, powerful, Holy Ghost revival preacher. For over 60 years, he has conducted evangelistic crusades across the United States and around the world.

R.W. Schambach's meetings are noted for enthusiastic worship, faith-building testimonies, and challenging, Bible-based sermons. His demonstrative preaching style and down-to-earth practical messages have endeared him to thousands of people who have found inspiration, encouragement, and deliverance in his services.

One of Brother Schambach's trademarks is the large Gospel tent utilized for so many city-wide and regional crusades. For many years, Brother Schambach took the "canvas cathedral" into inner-city locations where many preachers would not go to, where he attracted many people who would have never attended a typical church service.

Despite graduating from seminary and having various degrees conferred upon him, he is known simply as "Brother Schambach" to those to whom he ministers. Brother Schambach has tremendous compassion for people, often praying for them one at a time long after his services have ended.

Brother Schambach has personally conducted major open-air crusades and meetings in many countries across the globe, attracting some of the largest crowds ever assembled in the history of some nations.

Brother Schambach has also touched countless lives through television and radio ministry.

International headquarters for Schambach Ministries are located in East Texas. The ministry provides a "Power Prayer Line," receiving calls from people requesting prayer.

Thousands of Brother Schambach's sermons have been distributed on CD, DVD, VHS, and in book form.

R.W. Schambach and his wife, Mary Winifred, were married in 1948. They have three children. His daughter, Evangelist Donna Schambach, preaches and serves in the ministry together with him.

To contact the author, write:

Schambach Ministries
PO Box 9009
Tyler, TX 75711
Telephone: 903-825-9572

When You Need Prayer

Call the Power Phone

Every day of the week, a dedicated, faith-filled,
Bible-believing prayer partner is ready to talk with
you and pray about your needs.
When you need prayer call:

Phone: 903-825-9361

Additional copies of this book and other book titles from DESTINY IMAGE are available at your local bookstore.

Call toll-free: 1-800-722-6774.

Send a request for a catalog to:

Destiny Image® Publishers, Inc.

P.O. Box 310
Shippensburg, PA 17257-0310

"Speaking to the Purposes of God for this Generation and for the Generations to Come."

For a complete list of our titles, visit us at www.destinyimage.com.